ASTROLOGY
FOR TEENS

Understanding Your Connection To The Universe and Finding Your Place Among The Stars

Anne Bullock

ISBN: 978-1-962496-00-1

For questions, please reach out to Support@OakHarborPress.com

Please consider leaving a review!
Just visit: OakHarborPress.com/Reviews

FREE BONUS

SCAN ME!

GET OUR NEXT BOOK FOR FREE!

Scan or go to:
OakHarborPress.com/Free

Table of Contents

CHAPTER ONE: INTRODUCTION

Astrology is an exciting practice that people have been using for hundreds of years to better understand themselves and the world around them. While most people generally know what astrology is, there are few who can count themselves as experts on the practice. This book provides an introduction to astrology that will help you understand the deeper concepts and practices you can use to enrich your life in numerous ways.

WHAT IS ASTROLOGY?

Think about the last time you gazed at the stars. When it's dark and clear outside, you've probably tried to connect the dots of constellations in the sky. This can be a fun game, but for astrologers, the stars are not a game—they're a way of understanding. While you might not know a lot about astrology yet, anyone who has ever read a horoscope or talked about their zodiac sign already has some familiarity with astrological practice.

However, astrology is so much more than just your star sign or a way to predict your future. With a name that stems from Latin roots meaning "study of the stars," astrology is a profound metaphysical practice that connects celestial objects to human life. Astrology is not just one practice; it's a collection of behaviors used by cultures across the world and across the centuries. From ancient Greece to modern-day America, astrology has had many roles in academics, culture, literature, and religion, and it continues to be a prevalent part of human life.

For decades, people have used the heavens to tell stories and find meaning in the world, and you can be part of that long tradition through the practice of astrology. Ultimately, astrology embraces the stars and planets to foretell the future, explain the universe, and bring people like you closer to their true purposes. The stars are waiting to give you answers.

IS ASTROLOGY REAL?

Whether or not astrology is real is widely debated. There are many diehard believers and just as many skeptics. Astrology is no doubt real in that people around the world practice it and it adds meaning to many people's perspectives on human existence.

It's up to you to weigh the information and determine whether astrology is "real" to you. You have the chance to decide how you'll incorporate astrology into your life.

Some people like to learn about astrology to find a new way of looking at the world, while others get into astrology for something fun to do. Whether you're just curious about astrology or are already committed to it, it never hurts to learn more about this practice and how you can use it in your life.

No matter what you believe about astrology, you should remember that astrology is not certain, meaning that your horoscope or star sign won't commit you to any single fate. With or without the practice of astrology, you still have the power to make decisions and create a future that will bring you the greatest possible happiness and success. The stars can guide you, but they do not define you.

IS ASTROLOGY A SCIENCE?

One of the most fascinating parts of astrology is that it bridges physical sciences and metaphysical studies. Astrology relies both on spiritual and scientific ideas to create a well-balanced field that appeals to people of all backgrounds.

Much of astrology is about understanding the natural world, which is a common focus in scientific areas such as geology and biology. However, astrology not only seeks to discover the natural world but also tries to explain it through the movement of celestial bodies like the stars, moon, and sun. It uses the scientific knowledge of when celestial bodies will be in the sky to shape its beliefs. These qualities make astrology seem very scientific, yet it doesn't quite fit into a traditional scientific mold.

Astrology has some scientific tendencies, but it's more spiritual or transcendent than conventional natural sciences, meaning that it focuses on more than just what you can see, taste, touch, feel, or hear. Science focuses on the natural world, but practices like astrology seek to understand things we cannot—or cannot only—physically sense. Science, on the other hand, uses experiments and research to understand our experience in the natural world, but it rejects anything that goes beyond what we can physically sense and measure.

While astrology isn't the same as science, that doesn't mean it can't work alongside scientific understanding. Just as religious beliefs can coexist with scientific ones, astrology doesn't argue that science is wrong; it just poses the idea that our connection to the universe goes beyond the boundaries of science.

HOW IS ASTROLOGY DIFFERENT FROM ASTRONOMY?

Astrology and astronomy not only sound similar, but they also deal with similar topics using different approaches. Both study celestial bodies, but astronomy does so as a true science. Astrologers seek to understand the abstract and divine applications of celestial bodies, while astronomers use the scientific method to understand the physics of these bodies.

Although they're different fields, these areas of study do sometimes overlap. In early times, there was little distinction between the two because scientific studies had not advanced that far. But even in modern times, these two areas remain connected. For example, astronomers often refer to astrological constellations because the terminology is well known. While astronomers don't look at constellations in the same way as astrologers, there's still some harmony between the two belief systems.

IS ASTROLOGY RELIGIOUS?

There's no doubt that astrology is associated with spirituality, but it's not a religion on its own. However, some people use it as part of their religion or in addition to their religious beliefs. In fact, astrology has strong connections to ancient Chinese religion, and the zodiac is associated with Taoism. Among modern-day Christians, the popularity of astrology has waxed and waned, but early Christians commonly used astrology. It was highly popular during the Renaissance. However, many people who don't subscribe to any religion at all have also followed astrology. Thus, astrology can fit into the lives of religious and nonreligious people alike.

A BRIEF HISTORY OF ASTROLOGY

There are many books dedicated to the long and rich history of astrology. You don't need to know all the details of this history, but learning the major milestones does help to understand astrology's general roots and how the practice has evolved.

The origins of astrology can be traced to about 2000 BCE in Babylonia, where astrological charts were used to understand the seasons and celestial events. These practices helped people make seasonal predictions and probably feel less anxious about the future, which was filled with many uncertainties. During this era, astrology and astronomy were one and the same, and they would remain that way for over 2,000 years.

In the 4th century BCE, the Greeks learned astrology from the Babylonians. The Greeks' practice of astrology helped spread and immortalize the earlier Babylonians' understanding of astrology. The Greeks advanced the field by assigning the signs places on the zodiac wheel that's still in use today.

Among the ancient Greeks, noteworthy scholars began to speak highly of astrology, which helped lend it greater credibility. Aristotle and Plato are examples of prominent scholars whose understandings of the world were influenced by astrology. Hippocrates, for whom the Hippocratic Oath is named, claimed, "A physician without a knowledge of astrology has no right to call himself a physician." The significance of astrology in society had become undeniable.

Once astrology reached the Greeks, it spread quickly around the world. Soon Romans and people across the Arab world began to use astrology in their daily lives. People turned to astrology to make daily decisions of all kinds. While today we look to the internet when we have questions, our ancestors looked to the stars. In fact, they used astrology in nearly every area of their lives including agriculture, weather, and wartime strategy. Even kings and emperors trusted astrology. Scientists like Copernicus, Galileo, and Isaac Newton thought that astrology was science for the soul.

Throughout the years, the significance and usage of astrology has waxed and waned, but it has never died out. While astrology was long upheld as a crucial area of academic study, its prominence fell during the 17th century with the advent of modern astronomy and other scientific areas. As new knowledge and technology emerged and began to take precedence, astrology lost its reputation as a valid academic field and instead was deemed a pseudoscience. Although astrology no longer enjoyed the same level of credibility, it still maintained a place in societies around the world.

By the 20th century, astrology had regained some of its popularity, especially as it emerged in the consumer market. Newspaper horoscopes became common, making zodiac references household terms. Astrological practices and predictions became particularly popular during times of uncertainty such as the Vietnam War.

In the 21st century, astrology continues to be well known. During challenging times like the Great Recession of 2008, astrology has brought comfort and reassurance. Furthermore, the prominence of social media and concerning issues like the pandemic and the climate crisis have brought astrology into the current age. Modern technology has expanded people's ability to understand and engage with astrology. Apps and calculators allow people to know their charts quickly and effectively. It's never been easier or more meaningful to connect with astrology.

ASTROLOGY IN EVERYDAY LIFE

With millions of professional astrologers in the United States alone, it's clear that the practice of astrology is still thriving. You've probably had someone ask you what your sign is, and such an question is considered a normal social encounter, even if some consider astrology a game more than a serious practice. Astrology has been a part of human life for hundreds of years, and few things exist that long without maintaining some importance in everyday life.

Mythology has long been a part of human behavior and understanding, and astrology is one of the most powerful ways to engage with mythology. By telling stories using the stars, people can speak to true parts of humanity in ways that are broadly understandable. Astrology uses many mythological stories to celebrate the human drive for storytelling while striving to decode the universe's mysteries.

There's no doubt that astrology has influenced your life in some way. Whether you realize it or not, it's likely that many things you have learned about in school are influenced by astrology simply because it's so deeply ingrained in human culture and history. Science, history, philosophy, and psychology are just a few examples of academic areas that have been influenced by this field. For example, renowned psychoanalytical thinker Carl Jung believed that astrology could enable humans to know themselves better and help psychologists unpack the human psyche.

Big moments in history can all be explained by the heavens, and in uncertain times, people often looked to the stars, knowing there's so much more to life than what science can explain.

Various historical events show the dominance of astrology in our everyday mindsets. In the 1960s, for instance, when there was a lot of turbulence across the world, people turned to astrology and Eastern thinking to challenge the status quo and fight oppression. Amid the civil rights movement, anti-war protests, the fight for feminism, and general societal rebellion, more people trusted the stars to give them answers that established forces could not provide.

While different eras and cultures have featured different applications of astrology, many of its central elements remain fairly consistent. For example, Chinese culture recognizes 5 zodiac elements, and years are represented by 12 animals. Even though the Chinese zodiac looks very different from the one that's most familiar in the U.S., there is a great deal of overlap between the two, which attests to the relevance of these concepts across cultures.

Teens and young adults are starting to revive the study of astrology as they realize spirituality and scientific thought can coexist. Astrology is emerging as an area of interest, and #astrology has billions of views on social media, reflecting its recent growth in popularity.

CHAPTER TWO: ZODIAC SIGNS

Zodiac signs are the foundation of astrology. For hundreds of years, people have been using these signs to figure out how the world works. Zodiac signs and their interpretations have evolved over time, but the basic underlying concepts have remained the same throughout human history.

WHAT ARE ZODIAC SIGNS?

Chances are you've at least heard of zodiac signs before. If you've made a chart, you can probably identify your own sign and the signs of people you're close to. But don't assume there isn't more to learn. By understanding your zodiac sign and the signs of others, you can find a connection with the cosmos and seek a greater understanding of the universe. Being human is full of mystery and uncertainty, but zodiac signs offer clarity amid that complexity.

WHAT ARE ZODIAC SIGNS USED FOR?

The word *zodiac* actually comes from the Greek word meaning "circle of animals." The zodiac was initially created by Egyptians and Babylonians before being refined over hundreds of years. The original zodiac used the time it took for the sun to get back to its initial starting point (what we now identify as one year) and broke that cycle into 12 parts. The parts could then be used to keep track of time, which enabled people to better adapt to seasonal changes.

The zodiac signs are a guide and foundation for other astrological practices. The zodiac is usually presented as a sphere with the 12 different signs of the zodiac representing the 12 parts of the sky. Zodiac signs, also known as star signs, are thought to correlate with different traits, perspectives, strengths, and weaknesses.

BREAKING DOWN MISCONCEPTIONS

There are a lot of misconceptions about what zodiac signs are and how they work. To practice astrology effectively, it's important to unpack those misconceptions. By tackling these myths, you will gain the complete understanding you need to actually use zodiac signs rather than just knowing about them in a vague sense.

Misconception #1: Your Zodiac Sign Makes Up Your Whole Personality

If you're wondering how your zodiac sign could possibly determine your whole personality, you aren't alone. It's intimidating to think that your personality is defined by the date you were born. However, a zodiac sign doesn't define you entirely. The zodiac is never as simple as a math equation where $1 + 1 = 2$. It's much more abstract, and interpreting the zodiac requires additional understanding, nuance, and context.

Misconception #2: You Only Have One Sign

When someone asks you what your zodiac sign is, they're usually asking about your sun sign, but as you'll learn in future chapters, you also have other signs that help determine different parts of your personality and your future. Thus, even if you're born within a few days of someone else, you're likely very different from that other person. Signs such as your rising sign also influence who you are and how you engage with the world.

Misconception #3: Your Zodiac Sign Only Matters for Your Horoscope

Of course, horoscopes are very related to zodiac signs, but your zodiac sign can be used for much more. Different types of astrology use different methods. Horary astrology uses yes-or-no questions to ask what will happen during certain seasons, showing there are many versatile applications of your zodiac sign.

Misconception #4: There's Only One True Zodiac Interpretation

There are many different methods of interpretation that astrologers use to understand the zodiac. Because the zodiac gives so much information, many scholars focus on only a few areas. This is similar to seeing different types of doctors for different illnesses. For example, you may trust a cardiologist to know a lot about your heart, but you'd rather go to a dermatologist if you're having problems with your skin. Both can be equally qualified while having very different areas of expertise. The same can be said for astrologers, who may specialize in different interpretations of the zodiac.

Misconception #5: The Zodiac Is Too Simple to Be Useful

Skeptics say there's no way the zodiac can give people so much information with something as simple as the time you were born, but as discussed earlier, astrology is so much more than one zodiac sign. Scholars study astrology for years and still have a lot left to learn about this practice. Something that takes that much study is never simple.

Misconception #6: The Zodiac Is Occult

The occult refers to magical practices, but generally speaking, the zodiac is not occult. Some practitioners of the occult may also use the zodiac as part of their work, but the zodiac is not witchcraft and does not include casting spells. It's a mystical divination system that helps us understand the world based on what the universe is telling us.

Misconception #7: Your Zodiac Sign Dooms You

Your zodiac sign never means that you are doomed to any one fate. You still have the ability to make choices and define how you want to live your life. Astrology is a guide, but the more you mature, the more you will be able to use intuitive information to make decisions.

OVERVIEW OF THE 12 ZODIAC SIGNS

The 12 signs of the zodiac are linked to different abilities and struggles. They also relate to how you see other people and the world around you. While you only have one sun sign, you also have moon and planet signs, which may be different than your sun sign. Each sign in your overall birth chart can influence your characteristics and your future.

The Twelve Signs

- Aries
- Taurus
- Gemini
- Cancer
- Leo
- Virgo
- Libra
- Scorpio
- Sagittarius
- Capricorn
- Aquarius
- Pisces

Being familiar with all these signs is a must if you want to have a deep understanding of astrology. While some signs will impact your life more than others, all signs play some role in who you are and what your future holds.

Is There a 13th Sign?

For the purposes of this book, you don't have to worry about a 13th sign, but if you're doing independent research, you may stumble on a sign called Ophiuchus. This sign was identified after NASA affirmed that the sun moves through 13, rather than 12, constellations. However, prominent astrologers have argued against including this additional sign.

Ancient astrologers did acknowledge the existence of Ophiuchus, but the father of modern astrology, Ptolemy, determined that including it in the zodiac would ruin the balance of the calendar.

There are rare types of astrology that do use this constellation, but it's not common and, accordingly, won't be included in this book.

HOUSES, PLANETS, AND RULERS

In astrology, you'll commonly hear the terms *houses*, *planets*, and *rulers*. These terms allow better identification and understanding of the signs and how they interact with each other.

Planets, which include celestial bodies like the moon and the sun, are used to track key planetary bodies in astrology. The planets are used for both zodiac signs and houses, which are ways to interpret planetary movement and key parts of horoscopes and birth charts.

Each zodiac sign is assigned a planet, and that planet is understood to have a greater degree of influence over that sign. The planet is known as a *ruler* because it rules over the sign. While initially the zodiac only used seven celestial bodies, many other planets have since been discovered, which led to updates for some of the signs. For example, Uranus was assigned to Aquarius and Neptune was assigned to Pisces once those planets were discovered.

Astrology also uses house systems to interpret planetary connections. There are 12 houses on a wheel. The astrological houses govern various areas of life, so they're vital in any astrological reading. While houses are related to zodiac signs, these are slightly different. Zodiac signs are each associated with a house that takes on the same characteristics as the sign, but houses follow the Earth's one-day rotation rather than the sun's yearly path across the sky.

To put this into perspective, the first house on the wheel is ruled by Aries, but each person also has their own individual first house that depends on their birth chart. Your personal first house is overseen by your rising sign. Each house is presided over by signs based on your birth chart. Moreover, each house refers to certain characteristics. For example, the seventh house is all about balance. Like the zodiac signs, each house can give you different information about yourself.

You'll often see signs and houses swapped out interchangeably in many articles, but keep in mind that houses share characteristics of the sign that overrules them while operating independently. Both houses and signs share a connection with the planets. Ultimately, it is the planets that connect all these components of astrology and allow people to interpret this information.

PERSONALITY TRAITS OF EACH SIGN

Understanding the characteristics and personality traits of each sign not only allows you better understand yourself, but it can also inform your views on friends and family. You'll be able to act more collaboratively and gain insight into why others act the way they do. It's no wonder that psychologists have often been fascinated by astrology: Both practices study why people are the way they are and how to bring out positive qualities over negative ones.

Aries

Those born between March 21 and April 19 are in the first house of the zodiac, Aries. Aries is ruled by Mars, which matches this sign's fiery and passionate personality.

Known as "the ram," the Aries personality is filled with ambition. These people know what they want and aren't afraid to challenge themselves. They give their all to anything they do. If you're an Aries, you probably love competition in all forms. Aries people want to be the best, and they're willing to give their all to succeed. They stick to what they start. This shows in their relationships, too, as Aries are deeply loyal.

Aries have many gifts, but they also face particular challenges. While they are independent and forge their own paths, they tend to be impatient. They want to get started with tasks right away and see immediate results. They can be quite stubborn, so getting an Aries to change their mind is an uphill battle. Another challenge they face is taking it easy. They're so driven to be active that relaxing can seem difficult.

Taurus

Anyone born from April 20 to May 20 is a Taurus. Taurus is ruled by Venus and is represented by a bull, showing these people's firmness of opinion and confidence in what they believe.

Bulls are known for being unmoving, but that's not always the case. A Taurus will listen to the opinions of others, but they aren't going to pander to people, and they stay true to their own values even when other people pressure them to act in certain ways. A Taurus works hard to create their path and is known for being a trailblazer. They are choosy about who they let in their lives, opting for people who will be there for the long haul. They always want to make people they love feel confident.

One of the biggest challenges Taurus personalities face is that they aren't always hardworking. They are internally driven, so when external forces try to force them into something, they may become lazy and refuse to do that work. This can be challenging when they're trying to complete schoolwork or other activities that may not align with what the Taurus wants to be doing.

Gemini

With birthdates from May 21 to June 20, Geminis usher in the summer. Ruled by the planet Mercury and represented by twins, Geminis are known for being two sided and contain a lot of duality in their personalities.

These "twins" are fantastic at blending into their environments because they have different sides to show people depending on the situation. They know how to communicate well, which allows them to easily fit into groups. Their dynamic nature means that not only are they socially well versed, but they also have high emotional intelligence. Geminis are full of energy and always looking forward to the future and the next thing to do. They are great by themselves and in crowds.

Unfortunately, outsiders tend to see Geminis as two-faced because they can present differently in different situations. Their energy can be overwhelming, and Geminis may be more prone than other signs to gossiping. Their skills may frequently lead them to the middle of conflicts. Fortunately, Geminis are good at taking struggles in stride and not letting past conflicts ruin their futures.

Cancer

Represented by a crab, Cancers are born from June 21 to July 22. Their ruling planet is actually not a planet at all; they are represented by the moon as their chief celestial body, highlighting their depth as people.

Cancers are one of the most emotional signs, and they have so much emotional intuition that it may seem almost supernatural. While Cancers may seem hard to approach at first, when you get to know them, they are committed and share themselves deeply with other people. Cancers often see themselves as psychic and feel they have a greater connection with the universe. They are emotionally aware, but they're not going to beat around the bush or waste time on small talk.

Being emotional is often a strength for Cancers. However, this trait can backfire if they bottle up their emotions and then explode at something small. They may also assume that other people automatically know what they're thinking without defining their thoughts. Their inability to deal with conflict results in them struggling to give their opinion on matters that are likely to be contentious.

Leo

Leos are born from July 23 to August 22, and their ruling celestial body is the sun, matching their hot identity as proud and bold lions.

As a courageous sign, Leos aren't afraid to take a stand. They believe in themselves and are proud of what they do. When there is any injustice, Leos want to fight it. They also aren't shy about attention and love to be appreciated for their efforts. However, Leos don't rely on the recognition of others and are happy to give praise to themselves when they've done well. Leos are full of energy and intensity, and they know exactly what they want.

For all their good traits, Leos may struggle to listen or exert their power rather than offering gentleness. Leos also tend toward selfishness because of their strong awareness of their own wants. Their confidence can even border on arrogance. Fortunately, when Leos learn to regulate these negative traits, they can be fantastic leaders.

Virgo

Virgos, known as "the virgin," include all people who are born between August 23 to September 23. They are most known for being kind and full of grace. They are ruled by Mercury.

If an advice columnist were any one sign personified, they would be a Virgo. Virgos love to give advice and help people out whenever they can. While they are emotionally aware, they are also practical, so they don't get too lost in their feelings. Virgos are full of love and love beauty, but they live well-planned lives and it can take a while to be accepted into their neatly ordered worlds. However, they are incredibly passionate when you get to know them. Virgos are highly physical, especially in romantic relationships, and they love physical connection.

Unfortunately, Virgos tend to be perfectionistic. They can become rigid and may hold themselves and other people to unrealistic standards, which can cause unhappiness and friction in relationships. While they can be generous, they can also become frustrated when their expectations aren't met. Their drive to follow a schedule and make everything right may slow them down and make it hard for them to accept unexpected issues that arise.

Libra

Libras, represented by scales, are born between September 23 and October 22. They seek harmony and balance in all areas of life. Ruled by Venus, they also appreciate beauty and love.

If you're looking for a diplomat, you've found one in a Libra. Libras are always keeping the peace, and since they excel at seeing the world from other people's perspectives, they're useful in large groups where they can balance multiple personalities. Libras are dreamers, and they commonly think up plans, which makes them prone to artistic endeavors. They're big-picture people, and they don't like to be too focused on any one part of a pursuit. Restoring balance is always their goal when working on projects.

Libras dream big, but they don't always bring their dreams to life because they tend to struggle with a wandering mind. While they project a confident appearance, Libras can become insecure and may face existential doubts about who they are. They may struggle to understand their internal world, which can lead to a lot of distress. Libras can hurt themselves when they choose to do what makes other people happy rather than listening to what's best for themselves.

Scorpio

Scorpios are born from October 23 to November 21, and their ruling planet can be Pluto or Mars. Represented by the scorpion, Scorpios can seem intimidating to be around at first, but they can also be great allies.

While Scorpios can seem aloof or closed off, they open up to people they know and respect authenticity in others. Biting remarks and witty comebacks are common among Scorpios, and they love debating issues; sometimes, they'll take the most controversial opinion just for the sport of it. Scorpios can stand on their own, but when they are with people they know well, they are extremely loving and trustworthy.

Watch out for Scorpios because, while they make a great best friend, they make a terrifying enemy. Scorpios can become uncaring and cold to those who betray them, and outsiders may be afraid to approach them. Scorpios also struggle to show their emotions. They may force themselves to maintain a tough exterior and act as if they don't care rather than acknowledging and addressing their feelings, but that doesn't mean they aren't sensitive or don't care deeply.

Sagittarius

If your birthday is November 22 to December 21, your sign is Sagittarius and you are ruled by Jupiter. Sagittarians are represented by the archer, a testament to their strong-willed and adventurous demeanors.

Some people are born to lead, and that's the case with Sagittarians. They aren't afraid of trying novel things and are always trying to discover new parts of life to appreciate. They are honest to the core and love to open themselves up to others. Sagittarians would rather hurt someone than tell a lie, so they're great if you're looking for an honest opinion. They also tend to be great actors because they have big imaginations, which allow them to imagine what it would be like to be another person. Plus, they love the challenge that activities like acting bring.

The honesty that Sagittarians offer can sometimes lead to them seeming unempathetic to other people. They may come off as harsh and may be so independent that they end up being lone wolves rather than part of a group. However, they often have much better results when they are part of a group and can embrace their leadership skills, recognizing that they're better off sharing than keeping to themselves.

Capricorn

Capricorns are born between December 22 and January 19, and they're ruled by the planet Saturn. Represented by a goat, Capricorns can be stubborn, but they'll go the distance if you work with them.

If you're looking for someone smart with attention to detail, a Capricorn is the ideal choice. Hardworking and determined, if a Capricorn doesn't know how to do something, they'll learn. They're great at cultivating new skills, and they often know a little something about everything. Capricorns are clear about what they want and will seek out their desires however they can. They tend to be more constrained than other signs and appreciate traditions. Routine is a comforting force in their lives that keeps them organized.

Capricorns' stubbornness can get them into a lot of trouble. They are prone to expecting too much of themselves and other people, which can cause them to hold grudges and get upset when people can't meet their impossible standards. While they are intelligent and hardworking, they are often impeded by closed-minded thinking, and it takes a concentrated effort for them to see the bigger picture and understand how empowering an open mind can be.

Aquarius

Dubbed "the water bearer," Aquarius represents people born between January 20 and February 18. Aquarians are represented by Uranus and known for being intuitive, imaginative, and idealistic.

Unique is a word commonly used for Aquarians. Aquarians embrace their individuality and don't care if they're a little different than other people in their groups. Aquarians often want to promote big causes and see themselves as part of a greater chain of humanity. They are socially aware, and they take action to make positive changes. Their sincerity means that they speak from the heart, and while they can be a little quirky, they can accomplish big things.

Aquarians have strong values, which can sometimes lead them to act in ways that send the wrong message to other people. For example, an Aquarian may seem dismissive after canceling a date because a friend needs help with something. They can struggle to communicate appropriately to address any issues that may arise. Their uncompromising nature means they may be too rigid in what they believe, and they can be so focused on making the world better that they can lose sight of individual relationships.

Pisces

Born from February 19 to March 20, Pisces is the final sign in the zodiac, represented by a fish. Pisces is ruled by Neptune, reflecting their deep, intuitive abilities.

Intelligence, creativity, and intuition are key attributes of Pisces. They are known for being so intuitive they border on being psychic. Their imaginations allow them to come up with stories and new ideas. While they aren't always quick workers, they often come up with impressive results through their innovative methods. They're likely to have a unique process and enjoy the time spent coming up with ideas as much, if not more, than the process of bringing those ideas to life.

While strengths in many ways, their strong intuition and connection to the universe can be hard on Pisces. If you're a Pisces, you may feel emotions intensely and be really driven by your feelings, which can greatly impact your mood and mental state. Pisces tend to overthink think and catastrophize situations, so they become distraught, thinking that they can't fix a bad situation. Rather than sharing their troubles, they can keep them bottled up and struggle to be open with others to get the love and affection they so desperately want.

CHAPTER THREE:
THE SUN, MOON,
AND RISING SIGNS

It's time to explore some of the complexities of your birth chart. We're going to break down the most important information from the chart so that you can understand what it all means and how it applies to your life.

The Three Most Important Components of a Birth Chart

People are so different from one another, which makes it impossible to believe that personalities could be defined based only on 12 signs. Astrology accounts for these differences through the birth chart. Your sun sign may be your "main" zodiac sign, but you also have many other signs associated with celestial bodies. Each body dictates an individual part of your entire self. For instance, your sun sign is a general idea of who you are and what your destiny is, but your other signs show the more complex nuances of your personality.

Therefore, astrology acknowledges that there are depths to our personalities. For example, while you may seem bright and cheery to other people, a hidden part of you may have emotional struggles. These depths are what makes you a unique person. Because various parts of you are represented by different signs in your birth chart, there's nearly endless information you can discover when you study astrology.

Sun, moon, and rising signs are known as the big three types of signs in astrology because they're the celestial signs most often used in readings. You cannot calculate your moon or rising signs based on your sun sign alone. Thus, while your sun sign may be Aquarius, your rising sign could be Virgo. A Taurus with a moon in Libra will be very different than a Taurus with a moon in Cancer.

You may be tempted to try learning all your astrological placements right away, but that can be overwhelming, so starting with just these three chief signs will give you a strong foundation for astrology while still providing a range of information. Each type of sign will give you new and exciting insights about yourself, and by expanding your knowledge beyond just your sun sign, you'll unlock more astrological potential and create a base for further study.

THE TOP SIGNS IN YOUR CHART

Your sun, moon, and rising signs dictate different parts of your personality, and it's time to understand what each of these signs means.

Sun Sign

You already know a good bit about your sun sign and the sort of traits linked to the 12 sun signs. This sign is determined by the date of your birth. Most of what you already know about astrology is likely through the lens of your sun sign. Your sun sign corresponds to your conscious mind, and it is the most dominant sign in your chart.

Your sun represents the overarching traits that influence who you are. Think of your sun sign as a general impression of your personality and a foundation for your more intricate traits. The sun is the brightest astrological body, so it relates to the part of you that shines into the world. Your sun sign also reflects your core values, ambitions, and sense of self.

Moon Sign

The sun is bright and bold, while the moon is more shadowy in nature. This sign is determined by where the moon was in the sky at the time, place, and date of your birth. The sun lights up the moon, but it doesn't always light up the whole moon. Sometimes, you see just a sliver of the moon in the sky. Thus, you can think of your moon sign as the shadowy part of your personality. Your moon sign represents your inner world and emotions. Your sun sign can highlight your moon sign traits in the right conditions, but moon-sign traits are often instinctual and unconscious.

Your moon sign is highly spiritual because it embodies the energy of your soul. By understanding your moon sign, you can learn more about your deepest desires and fears. Your moods and emotions are mostly dictated by your moon sign. Additionally, matters of intimacy and vulnerability are heavily impacted by your moon sign. Therefore, deeper connections to people and the universe can depend on your relationship with your moon sign.

Rising Sign

Whereas your moon sign represents the depths of your internal world, your rising sign, also known as your ascendant sign, dictates how you are seen by other people. Your rising sign is determined by your time of birth, so to know this sign, you need to know not just the date but also the hour and minute of your birth. Your ascendant represents the sign that was rising on the eastern horizon when you were born.

Your rising sign represents the way you present yourself, and it can sometimes serve as a mask for what's happening internally. For instance, you may present yourself as agreeable and polite, while your deeper desires may be rebellious and wild. Your rising sign has a lot of power over your outward behavior and sense of style. Sometimes, your rising sign can overpower the traits of your sun sign, so if your sun sign doesn't seem to align with your personality well, it could be because of the boldness of your rising sign.

THE INFLUENCE OF SIGNS IN DIFFERENT POSITIONS

The characteristics of each sign will be slightly different based on their placement in your chart. While an Aries sun sign is known for being passionate and energetic, if you have a Pisces sun sign with Scorpio rising and an Aries moon sign, you may be quieter outwardly. Instead, the passion related to Aries might be reflected in your innermost wants. Therefore, it's important to know how the characteristics of each zodiac sign act when they are in different positions.

Aries

Aries signs are known for being passionate and full of energy, which allows them to achieve great things.

Sun

Aries are often enthusiastic, courageous, and confident, but they also be short tempered, moody, and impulsive. Aries get restless when they aren't doing anything, so they always trying to stay active. They thrive on competition and enjoy a challenge.

Moon

Those with an Aries moon sign will have burning inner passions and desires. They may experience turbulent emotions and pent-up anger, but they'll also have childlike enthusiasm for the things that interest them. Those with an Aries moon crave action and desperately want to bring their big ideas to life, but they can be impeded by passions that sometimes burn out before they come to life.

Rising

Aries rising signs are commonly great leaders, and they come off to others as innovators who are full of ideas. They may seem naïve because they can be idealistic. Their risk-taking and independence can lead to them becoming self-consumed and to protect themselves, they may be outwardly brash and abrasive. However, they often hide a deeper, more vulnerable side.

Taurus

Those with Taurus signs in their chart tend to be driven by sensory factors that help them stay grounded.

Sun

With a wealth of patience, Taurus sun signs have a level head and they're known for being responsible and practical. However, Taurus sun signs can also be stubborn and reluctant to change their ways, and they can respond poorly to unexpected issues that arise.

Taurus sun signs like things a certain way, and it can be frustrating to try to compromise with them.

Moon

If your moon is in Taurus, your emotions are highly tied to your senses. You are tactile and love to find beauty in the world. Sensory stimuli can impact your feelings, and if you sense something unpleasant, you're more likely to be in a bad mood. Regardless, those with a Taurus moon sign are relatively calm, and they appreciate sensual pleasures like candles, warm baths, and beloved baked goods. People with this sign feel no need to rush because they like to spend moments appreciating what's around them.

Rising

Taurus rising signs seem like unmovable forces who are consistent in everything they do. They usually seem laidback, but this relaxed nature may not reflect their emotional states. You'll frequently see them appreciating luxury things in life. They often wear designer clothes or go to top-rated restaurants. Their association with Venus means they project beauty into the world and love to explore their personal style through clothes or interior design.

Although they like the good things in life, that doesn't mean those with Taurus rising signs can't also appreciate the beauty of simple wonders.

Gemini

Geminis are best known for their duality, meaning they can adapt to any situation, but the dueling parts of Geminis can also make them indecisive and unpredictable.

Sun

Those with a Gemini sun sign are like chameleons. At certain times, they can be unreliable, but for the most part, they are very affectionate toward people and have a gentle disposition. Their curiosity and adaptability help them achieve their goals.

Moon

Gemini moon signs are dynamic people. Just as the moon goes through its phases, so do Gemini moon signs. The duality of a Gemini moon cannot be understated, and people with this sign commonly have complex emotional experiences. They're full of thoughts and dreams, and these ideas can be mercurial. Those with Gemini moon signs may follow whims or have trouble staying in one place, but they are intellectual and independent.

Rising

If you have a Gemini rising sign, you're probably great in social situations. Even if you're an introvert, you're most likely still adept at fitting into any environment. People in this category love highly stimulating situations, and the challenge of flirting can be exciting for Gemini rising signs. Gemini rising signs can be fun to be around, but it may be harder to get to know them beneath the surface level because they're so adept at putting on social masks and blending in.

Cancer

Cancers are some of the most emotional of all the zodiac signs, which can make them sympathetic but overly dramatic from time to time.

Sun

People who have a sun in Cancer are determined, loyal, and sensitive. However, their highly emotional disposition can lead to Cancers having low self-esteem or being pessimistic. Their intense feelings can also heighten their manipulative tendencies. Cancers put their hearts above their heads, so they can get stuck in their emotions and struggle to look at things logically.

Moon

Those with a moon in Cancer are nurturing and sensitive, so you might find yourself wanting to help others if this is your moon sign. Cancer moons are highly emotional, but they tend to be content with their emotional sides. They don't mind crying when they're sad or even joyful. Expressing their emotions makes them feel revived. However, those with a Cancer moon sign may have a sun sign that makes them overly prone to bottling up their emotions rather than sharing their deepest thoughts and wishes. This tendency can lead to Cancer moon signs feeling emotionally frustrated.

Rising

Those with Cancer rising signs can be shy when you first meet them because it takes time to build trust and emotionally open up. People who are Cancer rising tend to be introverted and like to spend time at home. Although they're introverted, Cancer rising signs love to form close connections with people, and they offer nurturing and emotional caretaking to other people to show their love. Because Cancer rising signs can be more reactive to emotions, they require a lot of emotional security to feel safe. Like Pisces, they tend to be so intuitive that they can seem almost psychic. Their high emotional intensity can lead to them being needy and struggling to balance their emotions.

Leo

Leos are bold and confident in their skills. They are known for being dominant leaders and highly social.

Sun

If you have a sun in Leo, chances are you're a born leader. You've probably had people following your lead since you were a little kid. You have immense magnetism and love having fun. Leos can become arrogant and selfish, but these traits are often moderated by their rich social lives.

Moon

People who have a Leo moon sign are internally joyful and confident. Those with a Leo moon tend to be creative, and they are emotionally satiated by having an audience who can applaud their boldness. If you have a Leo moon sign, you may crave attention and do whatever it takes to get the attention you want. You may especially feel at home being on a stage. Leo moons can be incredibly warm and generous, but they do like to be the center of attention.

Rising

More than any other rising sign, Leos are the life of the party. Their bold personalities and extroversion make them a lot of fun. Being in the spotlight gives them a lot of energy. However, while they are often very confident, even bordering on arrogant, they do have insecurities. When they feel attacked or challenged, they're quite sensitive. They get angry when anyone tries to tell them to be quiet or says that they're wrong. They tend to be great leaders, but they can become overly aggressive and intimidating with their intensity. Leo rising signs may present themselves in a traditional Leo fashion, but they may have more intense doubts internally.

Virgo

Kind, analytical Virgos pay great attention to detail while also having a deep affection for humanity. They want to spread goodwill and love.

Sun

Sun signs in Virgo are meticulous in their pursuits, but they are not entirely rigid because they can show deep empathy and kindness. Although they strive to be kind, Virgos do tend to be overly critical and can work too much. They may heavily scrutinize their own work and the work of others. Some Virgos are also quite shy, so they might lack the boldness they need to make the impact they want.

Moon

Virgo moon signs tend to be emotionally influenced by logic. Virgos don't like to let their emotions take over, so they tend to try to keep their emotions in check. They are analytical and have a tendency to create and use systems that help them feel calm and collected. Unfortunately, their need for order can make them prone to excessive worry. Even with the use of logic, they can struggle to soothe their anxiety and maintain a sense of order in a chaotic world.

Rising

Those with a Virgo rising sign are always trying to discover more about themselves and the rest of the world. They go out of their way to not be a burden and always try to do things to help others. Virgo rising signs can be quite critical, which can create tense social situations because they don't always realize how they come across. Despite their judgmental side, people are drawn to those with a Virgo rising sign because it's easy to open up to them about hard topics. Virgo rising signs are often terrific listeners.

Libra

Libras play well with others, and they use their diplomatic skills to fight the injustice and chaos of the world.

Sun

Those with their sun in Libra love harmony and become uncomfortable when there's a lot of conflict. When they run into conflict, they may try to avoid confrontation despite wanting the situation to improve. Libras love to share their goodwill and desire for social justice with others. They thrive when there is peace. However, they are prone to indecision and holding grudges against people they think have wronged them.

Moon

Libra is all about balance, and those with a Libra moon sign often seek internal balance and peace. They love to work with others to reach emotional balance, and they find internal validation rather than seeking it from the outside world, which helps them follow their own paths. Libra moons are often charming because of their drive to avoid conflict. They are great at moderating extreme traits in others, making them wonderful partners. Libra moons are often quite calming for other people to be around.

Rising

You'll frequently see Libra rising signs trying to make peace. Their need for harmony makes them want to step in when there's conflict, but some people with a Libra rising sign may be afraid of confrontation. These fears can cause them to freeze in the face of chaos, making it hard for them to know what to do. Because they like to know they're making a good decision, you may notice that Libra rising signs tend to take a while to weigh out the pros and cons of a situation. When they've finished their calculations, they're confident in their decisions. They also succeed at working with others and are commonly part of large social groups. People in this category fit in well at social gatherings.

Scorpio

Scorpios are assertive and passionate, and their ability to focus means they dive into something of interest and keep going until they find the answers or results they want.

Sun

People with a Scorpio sun sign value honesty, and they are confident in their knowledge. They will do whatever it takes to get the results they want, and their resourcefulness makes them an intense adversary. You can't calm their passion, and while they may not have the same kind of bravery as Leos, they are scrappy and brave when challenged. They may struggle to trust people and become jealous easily, but once you are on their good side, Scorpio sun signs maintain deep friendships.

Moon

When you have a moon in Scorpio, you tend to keep your innermost thoughts and feelings private. It takes a lot for Scorpio moons to open up, but when they trust someone, they share deep thoughts and love to be introspective. Scorpio moons have intense emotions, so they often need to take steps to guard their mental health and establish boundaries with other people. Scorpio moons value loyalty, and they can be conniving or petty with people they don't like or trust. However, when this sign is someone's moon side, their pettiness might be more on the side of passive aggression.

Rising

Scorpio rising signs are more likely to keep to themselves. They seem more withdrawn from the outside. Scorpio rising signs can also be bitter and biting when someone gets on their wrong side. They can become possessive of friends and people in their relationships because relationships with a Scorpio rising tend to be intimate and intense. You must earn a place in the life of a Scorpio rising sign. They tend to be moody, but they protect those they love and don't give up on their friends.

Sagittarius

Those with Sagittarius sun signs are open minded and love social events; they explore their world with heaps of curiosity.

Sun

Sagittarians often have the best sense of humor. They have high energy levels and are more extroverted than many of the other signs. While they love being around other people, they can sometimes be impatient. They're often blunt, saying whatever they please without caring what other people think. They are idealistic, which means they can sometimes overpromise and underdeliver.

Moon

The curiosity of Sagittarius moons means they love deepening their intellectual knowledge. They love exploring and are emotionally enriched by endeavors that allow them a deeper understanding of how the world works. At times, they can become overly dominant and struggle to moderate themselves in conversation. They can become so excited that they talk over people without realizing it, and they may feel like they're smarter than others. However, when they can moderate those tendencies, they can be the life of the party.

Rising

Sagittarius rising signs will often be seen exploring new environments. They wander off looking for new adventures wherever they are, so you'll always see them trying new pursuits. They are extroverted in social situations, but they can get themselves in trouble when they give their opinions without holding back. Although they love to take big steps toward the future, they tend to be very present in whatever they are doing and don't mind taking risks to get ahead.

Capricorn

Capricorns are self-disciplined and embrace tradition, responsibility, and learning from their mistakes.

Sun

Of all the signs, Capricorn sun signs are the most connected to traditions. They value beliefs and behaviors that have been passed down through the generations. This doesn't mean they follow traditions that don't match their values, but they get fulfillment from the connection that tradition brings. Capricorns have strong self-control, which makes them quite serious and prone to using planning and management skills to get ahead.

Moon

Capricorn moons feel best when they are working hard and making things happen. Success will make Capricorn moons feel like they're in their element, and they may feel stifled when they aren't living up to their potential. Those with Capricorn moons benefit from setting goals and always having something to strive for; otherwise, they might struggle to regulate their emotions. While they love to work hard, Capricorn moons also know how to have a good time. At a party, they love to impress people with party tricks. However, their social interactions can become shallow as they often struggle to let others connect to their emotional sides.

Rising

Those with a Capricorn rising sign are often entrepreneurial, so you'll often see them trying to make more money. They love earning their success, and if you're a Capricorn rising, you probably have a go-getter attitude. Capricorn risings can come off as cold and overly driven, but they might have a softer core depending on their moon sign. Capricorn rising signs are always doing something, and they often present themselves based on traditions that have been passed through the generations. For

Capricorn rising signs, mistakes are not all that bad, but they are a chance to do better going forward.

Aquarius

Aquarians are the humanitarians of the zodiac, and while they come off as aloof, they love to advocate for the causes they believe in.

Sun

Those with a sun in Aquarius are often known for their eccentricities. They embrace their uniqueness and are heavily driven by their strong sense of humanity. They may give off a holier-than-thou vibe because of their strong moral compasses, and at times, they can refuse to compromise. Because of their temperamental moods, Aquariuans don't always seem approachable. However, they are always up for intellectual discussions and are very socially oriented.

Moon

People with a moon in Aquarius feel their emotions as something bigger than themselves. They see their feelings as part of a greater human struggle, and they are driven by trying to rectify injustices. They can be overly moral and become so consumed by doing the right thing that they lose sight of the people around them. Those with Aquarius moons must work to avoid becoming too fixated on their internal sense of right and wrong. It takes conscious effort for them to listen to others and form a meaningful connection.

Rising

With an Aquarius rising sign, you likely have some of the humanitarianism of Aquarians, so people might see you as someone who wants to help the world. You may also appear unique because you don't bend to the expectations or norms of others. Those with an Aquarius rising sign dedicate themselves to causes that make them feel passionate because they love being a part of the bigger universe. You'll commonly see these people participate in culture, arts, or language. They love to expand their view of the world and be a deeper part of society.

Pisces

Pisces are so intuitive that some might consider themselves to be psychic. They're highly connected to the spiritual universe around them, and this connection makes them wise and gives them a strong sense of compassion for others.

Sun

Those with a sun sign in Pisces are often introverted, but they have a lot of compassion and like creating strong connections with people. They can easily get lost in their own heads and may want to escape the hardships of their daily lives. They can become melancholic and get stuck in dark thoughts, but when they overcome this struggle, Pisces can be artistic and selfless.

Moon

With a moon in Pisces, a person may have intense emotions that correspond to the feelings of those around them. These people tend to be emotional sponges, so when they sense emotion from other people, they absorb it into themselves. Philosophical musings and daydreaming are common for those with a Pisces moon. While these people are old souls with deep thoughts, they can become overly contemplative, which can make it hard to be fully present in everyday activities.

Rising

Pisces rising signs are the people you always see stepping in to help. They are connected to the great parts of the universe, including animals, plants, and people. They aren't afraid to visibly show their emotions, so you can usually tell what Pisces rising signs are thinking. People in this group wear their hearts on their sleeves and have an earnest nature. However, they can get quite animated and struggle to listen to rational conversations because they are so driven by emotion.

CHAPTER FOUR:
THE ELEMENTS AND MODALITIES

Elements and modalities are another crucial part of understanding astrology because each sign has an element and modality associated with it. This chapter will unpack how these elements and modalities work together to shape the 12 astrological signs. You will also learn how to use them for better astrological analysis.

What Are the Elements and Modalities?

Many subdivisions can help you learn more about what your astrological signs mean and how to interpret them to find success and a deeper connection to the universe. Both the elements and modalities of astrology give you additional information that you'll be able to use in so many ways as you continue on your astrological journey.

ELEMENTS OF ASTROLOGY

The zodiac signs are divided into four elements. You're probably already familiar with the four elements that represent the different qualities inherent in the universe: earth, water, air, and fire. The elements in astrology are divided based on quadrants of the zodiac, which are split into subsections. Each quadrant is assigned three signs. The elemental associations show which signs correlate to different parts of the natural universe.

This chapter will go deeper into what each element means, but for now, try to remember which signs are associated with each of the four elements. The elements are referred to as *triplicities* because each element accounts for three signs.

Earth signs: Capricorn, Taurus, Virgo

Water signs: Cancer, Scorpio, Pisces

Air signs: Libra, Aquarius, Gemini

Fire signs: Aries, Sagittarius, Leo

While a certain element may be stronger in you based on your natal chart, each person has components of all four elements within them. Thus, if certain characteristics of other elements relate to you, that's perfectly normal. The combination of elements inside you can create disharmony or harmony, so being aware of the relationship between elements is useful information to have.

Elements tend to reflect your general disposition. Just like different elements of the universe are building blocks, the element of your sign also corresponds to the building blocks of who you are. Your elemental tendencies don't define how you will act, but they can influence what drives your behavior.

Earth

Earth is related to Capricorn, Virgo, and Taurus, so this element is also related to the second, sixth, and seventh houses of the zodiac. These signs are grounded and practical. Those ruled by the earth element tend to be reluctant to take risks because they prefer to do things they know will work out. People affiliated with this element always speak logically and often try to keep everyone else grounded in their friend groups.

Because of their association with the earth, those with earth element signs are often builders. They love to create something from nothing and work with their hands to get big results. While their urge to build drives them to success, it can also make them want too much. Earth signs can set their sights too high. They can also become overly consumed by sensory pursuits. Furthermore, they may judge other people who are not as grounded and struggle to understand those who take a more emotional perspective on life.

For all their faults, earth signs are some of the most dependable people you will meet. They're driven, and they have a connection to nature and anything they can build from the plentiful earthly goods around them.

Water

Those who are Cancers, Scorpios, or Pisces are water signs, so water signs correlate to the fourth, eighth, and twelfth houses of the zodiac. Water signs have a lot of depth. Like a river or an ocean, they are fluid and full of movement. They can be calm and tranquil, but when they are stormy, they can be incredibly intense. This duality comes from how sensitive and intuitive water signs are. While these signs may seem unassuming, you can never underestimate the power of water.

Due to their sensitive nature, water signs are great at caretaking and sharing deep feelings with other people, but they can easily become overwhelmed by their emotions. In settings where there are a lot of emotions from other people, they can struggle to cope with so much emotional energy. They tend to be brooding and prone to mood swings. However, when they learn to process their emotions, they are great at helping other people healthily deal with their feelings.

If you're a water sign, chances are that you love to be artistic and can find ways to turn all those feelings into something amazing. However, water signs have to be careful not to get lost in their creative worlds and remember there are other parts of life than just those deep emotions.

Air

Geminis, Libras, and Aquarians make up the air signs, which correlate to the third, seventh, and eleventh signs of the zodiac. Air signs are intellectuals, which means they love to analyze the world around them, and they are excellent at understanding abstract logical concepts. When you need a problem solved, the air signs will excitedly get to work finding the answers you need. They do well with challenges and can get bored when they aren't stimulated enough.

Communication is another important skill of air signs, but they hate small talk. They want to have deep, meaningful conversations. They can be good listeners and pick up on signals that other elemental signs may miss. Thus, they are quite perceptive, and their natural curiosity makes them want to dig deeper and always learn more. Air signs are great to be around and can be fantastic friends, but they can become like overpowering gusts of wind and turn things on their heads when they get upset. When they are teased or taunted, air signs can become cold and biting. Their temperaments can quickly change.

While they are scary as adversaries, when you are friends with an air sign, they are often humanitarians. They can clearly perceive how things are for other people and come up with creative, clever solutions for big problems. Their idealism makes them believe they can take on the world and drives them to always strive for more.

Fire

The fire signs include Aries, Leo, and Sagittarius, the first, fifth, and ninth houses of the zodiac. As you may expect, fire signs are full of passion. Their feelings are big, and their ambitions are even bigger. These people are commonly the life of the party, and many fire signs want to be the center of attention wherever they go. Their huge personalities are almost impossible to miss.

The passion and ambition of fire signs are often advantageous, but fire signs can also burn too brightly. It can be hard for them to control their wants and behaviors. If they aren't careful, they can spiral out of control and cause a lot of destruction. They can be demanding and seek control of situations. Their confidence can border on arrogance, but when they keep others at the forefront of their mind, they can be loyal and protective of those they love.

Fire signs can stand on their own two feet. They know how to be independent and strong. They are bold people, and they aren't afraid to resist societal norms to get what they want. They feel most alive when they are in action and can easily become bored when they don't have enough to do. Fire signs are fun to be around. They cannot be tamed, but for the most part, you won't feel the need to try.

MODALITIES IN ASTROLOGY

You can think of astrological modalities as the signs' modus operandi. While signs can be identified by what they are, the modalities help define how all the signs work. Each of the three modalities has four of its own signs. Because each modality has four signs, you may see these also referred to as *quadruplicates*.

Cardinal: Aries, Cancer, Libra, Capricorn

Fixed: Taurus, Leo, Scorpio, Aquarius

Mutable: Gemini, Virgo, Sagittarius, Pisces

The classification of modalities is distinct from the classification of elements, meaning that signs with the same elements don't necessarily have the same modalities. While elements express your core temperament, modalities are more indicative of how you will behave. Like any astrological concept, they don't doom you to certain behaviors, but they do create a stronger draw to particular patterns. Each sign is associated with the three life conditions: creation, preservation, and transformation.

The modalities are organized based on seasons. Each modality is represented in all four seasons. For example, in winter, Capricorn is cardinal, Aquarius is fixed, and Pisces is mutable. Modalities also correspond to night and day, so each modality has inhale and exhale signs. Inhale signs represent the day, while exhale signs represent the night.

Cardinal

The cardinal signs are Libra, Aries, Cancer, and Capricorn. These signs are at the beginning of each of the seasons in the quadrants of the zodiac. While Aries and Libra represent the day, Cancer and Capricorn represent the night. If most of your planets are in one of these houses, you will be more prone to cardinal tendencies.

Cardinal signs are known as "initiators" because they tend to create change. Their location on the zodiac wheel reflects this role because cardinal signs commence their seasons and get the gears going for projects. They are the people full of initiative, who are determined to bring to life their big dreams. Although they love to get things started, if they lose steam, cardinal signs may have trouble finishing a project. They love hard work, but because their ambition drives them, if they lose interest, they move onto other tasks. Thus, they work well with signs who can keep them on task and remind them of their big dreams.

If you're a cardinal sign, you're probably full of energy when you begin a project. Some people may even say that you're too energetic when you're in the zone. This tendency can make it challenging for cardinal signs to pay attention to the wants or needs of others. Fortunately, despite some tendencies toward self-centeredness, cardinal signs have an infectious energy.

Fixed

Fixed signs are in the middle of their seasons. Leo, Scorpio, Aquarius, and Taurus are all in this category. The exhale signs of this group are Taurus and Scorpio; the inhale the inhale signs are Aquarius and Leo. Being in the middle of the bold initiators and the flexible parts of the zodiac, fixed signs are the most anchored of all the modalities.

While cardinal signs have the big energy to get the ball rolling, fixed signs are the best at sustaining projects. Those with fixed signs won't give up easily when they set their minds to something. They're great at keeping their heads on straight and pushing themselves through the challenging parts of any task. It's actually the challenge that makes fixed signs so excited to get started on something, so if they aren't challenged, they may not see the point of working on a project. They are confident, self-driven, and know their purpose. Fixed signs never want to feel like they're wasting their time, and their deep concentration means they can easily handle huge responsibilities without a problem.

Those who have a lot of cardinal signs in their birth charts can be too stubborn for their own good. For example, idealistic Aquarians can be so passionate about accomplishing their dreams that they refuse to listen when anyone tries to slow them down. However, when they focus on their patient dispositions and keep even-keeled heads, they're reliable partners.

Mutable

The mutable signs are the last of their respective seasons. Gemini and Sagittarius are inhale signs, while Virgo and Pisces are exhale signs. These round out the zodiac and help put a nice little bow on the end of a chapter. Their tendency toward mutability means they are the most "go with the flow" of all the signs, and they choose free expression over rigidness.

The other groups may struggle when unexpected issues arise, but mutable signs embrace speed bumps and know how to adapt to whatever situation they're in. Their easygoing personalities allow them to focus on creativity and channel their imaginations in new ways.

Mutable signs are full of ideas, but they don't always bring them to fruition. They may need help from cardinal signs to get the ball rolling. However, they are great team members because they boost the mood of a group when bad things happen; they have a unique ability to turn a bad situation into an opportunity. They want to make everyone happy, so they aren't as decided as fixed or cardinal signs, which can make them appear two-faced or indecisive. Even so, their resourcefulness and ability to recover from nearly anything mean that when they fall, they know how to get back up.

HOW DO ELEMENTS AND MODALITIES INFLUENCE THINGS?

Elements and modalities are distinct parts of astrology, but they have been combined in this chapter because it's common to see elements paired with modalities. For instance, a Libra could say they're a cardinal air sign, while a Gemini is also an air sign but is a mutable one. These differences may seem small, but they transform how each person interacts with the world around them.

While it's common to focus on the modalities and elements of your sun sign, the elements and modalities of your other types of signs can also be impactful because they can help you unpack the different facets of your personality. For instance, while the modality of your sun sign represents how you generally behave when it comes to emotional matters, the modality of your moon sign can more closely define how you behave emotionally.

When using modalities and elements, you don't just want to look at individual signs—you also want to look at your chart overall. For example, if your chart contains a lot of earth signs, that suggests earth will play a significant role in your personality and will be a consistent thread throughout your decision-making.

However, if you have an even number of modalities or elements across your chart, you may be more likely to react differently in changing situations.

TRAITS OF EACH ELEMENT/MODALITY

Now it's time to combine both the elements and modalities to better delve into the dispositions and behaviors of each sign.

Aries

As a cardinal fire, Aries are passionate and all about starting new projects. The ram represents these confident trailblazers. They fight to be the best, and along with Leos, they are one of the most competitive of all the signs. Aries create their own paths because their fire element means they know their own passions. If they aren't totally committed, there's no way they'll ever attempt a task.

As a cardinal sign, Aries is the first one to work on a project. They can become disillusioned if the project doesn't go the way they want. If their passion dies down, they'll find something new. They commonly bounce around between projects because of their cardinal nature, but their fire elements mean they always have something in the works, and they'll strive to reach the top in whatever they do.

Taurus

Taurus is defined as a fixed earth, and this is a perfect combination for bulls. Tauruses are known for being stubborn, yes, but they are so much more than that thanks to their combination of modality and element. Their earth element means that they are more likely do so on a whim, but they're open to hearing new information and changing when they believe they were previously wrong.

The stubbornness of Taurus mostly comes from being a fixed sign. Fixed signs are known for diving into projects and sustaining their efforts. They aren't the type to give up once they've started something, and Tauruses combine this stubborn nature with their earthly qualities. Being associated with the Earth means that Tauruses know the value of hard work, and they aren't afraid to get dirty to complete a task.

Gemini

Often known for their duality, it's no wonder that Geminis are mutable air signs. They combine the intellectual and humanitarianism of air signs with the free-spirited, adaptable energy of mutable signs. This combination can make Geminis enigmatic, and it can take a while of knowing a Gemini to get to know the contrasting parts of their personality and characterization.

The two-faced reputation Geminis get comes down to the combination of their element and modality. Many aspects of Geminis don't quite make sense because they can conflict with each other, but with a deeper look, you can see how fascinatingly complex Geminis are. As a mutable sign, Geminis often are people-pleasers and social chameleons. They adapt to whatever situations they're in, which can make them great at dinner parties or on the dance floor, but this tendency can make some people think they're disingenuous.

Cancer

Emotional Cancers are cardinal water signs. This combination of facets means that Cancers have an emotional intensity that most other signs don't. They can get swept away by the waves of life and throw themselves into deep emotions with no way back to the surface. Even so, their emotional richness means they have great intuition.

Cancers have all the depths of water signs. They can be driven to moodiness by their emotional connection to the world, and they often yearn to push past shallow knowledge and understand the universe on a deeper level. The cardinal nature of Cancers means they're excited about starting projects, but they can quit before they finish. They lose that initial momentum, which is often related to the hard feelings they have. Cancers can get so trapped in their feelings that they struggle to follow through. However, when they learn to balance their emotional intensity, they are great caretakers who love to get involved with projects that benefit the Earth and its inhabitants.

Leo

Bold and confident, Leos are fixed fire signs. As fixed signs, Leos are great at continuing projects. They sustain projects and can breathe new life into tasks that others may have abandoned. Leos are perfectly represented by a lion. They have big voices and a lot of courage. Leos are confident, and there's never a doubt about what they're going after.

When Leos are committed, they don't back down. They're ready for a fight, and if you stomp all over their ego, you may get burned by this fiery sign. Leos are similar to Aries, but while Aries get the ball rolling, Leos are more likely to see a project through because of their fixed signs. They often like to have control over the entire project, so they may be prone to micromanaging in their attempts at being a great leader.

Virgo

Being so practical and systematic, it's no wonder that Virgos are mutable earth signs. Virgos are grounded perfectionists. While their perfectionist nature seems like it would conflict with the more free-flowing mentality of most mutable signs, Virgos have the resourcefulness to match. They are also people-pleasers, always wanting to adapt themselves to each situation to make others happy.

The amazing thing about Virgos is how they combine logic with flexibility. Other earth signs tend to struggle with flexibility or see life as very cut and dry, so the way Virgos process the world is unique. Likewise, Virgos are able to take in and process new details effectively, and they adapt themselves to reflect that information. They blend the free-flowing nature of mutable signs with the grounded practicality of earth signs.

Libra

As cardinal air signs, Libras are all about balance and they're great facilitators of communication. Libras love embracing community and serving as arbiters of justice, but they are also prone to other areas of balance. For example, appearance is also very important to Libras. They want the world to feel like it's in perfect order.

The cardinal nature of Libras means it's common to find them starting projects to promote diplomacy and improve interpersonal communication. However, Libras can struggle with confrontation, making it hard for them to follow through when they're met with pushback to their diplomatic efforts. Meanwhile, the air nature of Libras means they are creative problem solvers, and their aptitude for communication makes it easier to appease all parties involved in tense situations.

Scorpio

With their passion and strategic minds, many people mistake Scorpios for fire signs, but they are actually fixed water signs. As such, Scorpios combine an emotional, intuitive nature with a deep drive for completing big tasks. Once they get invested in something, Scorpios are fully in and there isn't much you can say to get them to quit. Sometimes, they'll keep going just to prove their determination even though they know the project isn't worth continuing.

Being a fixed sign, Scorpios never give up easily. They can become stubborn and unwilling to change their minds when they're already invested in something. Furthermore, as a water sign, Scorpios are full of depth. To them, life is a game of chess, and they're always trying to get to checkmate. They won't admit defeat if they don't have to. Like a scorpion, Scorpios will wait for the perfect moment to strike, and they can be quite sneaky, so their enemies are rarely prepared for what Scorpios have up their sleeves.

Sagittarius

Sagittarians are passionate and adaptable, so it checks out that they are mutable fire signs. Sagittarians are unique because they combine fiery passion and ambition with the more free-spirited nature of mutable signs. They love to find adventure in life, and being so curious, they'll dream up new things to try all the time.

Their friends may struggle to keep up with them, and their fire element means they can be so blunt and open about their thoughts that they can seem harsh. If you aren't ready for their honesty, miscommunication can cause a lot of trouble.

Because they have mutable signs, when things go wrong, Sagittarians don't let their passion die; instead, they learn to adapt to whatever challenge they're experiencing. They yearn for change and excitement, but they're not so set in their ways that they won't embrace the winding paths of life. Sagittarians will be blissful if you give them a chance to explore the world.

Capricorn

The responsible and steadfast Capricorn is sure to promote stability, driven by ambition and just a little mischief. This cardinal earth sign is not only great at getting projects started but also excels at staying grounded throughout the process without becoming too prideful or arrogant. When you meet a Capricorn, they are commonly quite restrained at first; they may even seem dull. However, as you get to know Capricorns, you can see that there's so much more than just a responsible person. Being responsible doesn't mean Capricorns don't like to have fun, and it's common for them to have little moments of mischief.

Capricorns are energized by being able to make something out of nothing. Both the cardinal and earth parts of this sign make Capricorns desire to build from the earth and start big projects. The grounded nature of Capricorns means they're not only good at dealing with the material world, but they're also in tune with the emotional energies around them.

Aquarius

Aquarians are fixed air signs who love to partake in projects that better society. Humanitarians at heart, Aquarians are prone to being sanctimonious, but it's only because they are so committed to whatever causes they choose. They are great at working to build communities. By combining a fixed sign with an air sign, you get a dedicated and committed person who will put tireless energy into digging deep and getting positive results. Because Aquarius is represented by a water bearer, people often think they are water signs, but if you know an Aquarius, it'll be clear that they're really an air sign.

Aquarians are the last air sign in the zodiac, which means they deal with air from a bigger-picture perspective. Driven by air, Aquarians are deeply intellectual, so when you converse with them, you may notice that they choose intellectual conversations and debates over small talk. They think big and want to help the whole world. Their fixed nature means that they might not listen when you try to tell them they're wrong, and once they start something, they'll struggle to pay attention to other things.

Pisces

As a mutable water sign, Pisces are artistic with lots of depth. They are one of the moodiest signs. Their fluidity allows them to be flexible in a variety of situations, embodying their mutable nature. They are imaginative, and they love to explore the world in new ways. For Pisces, looking at just the surface of a situation isn't enough.

They are highly intuitive and always trying to go deeper into their feelings and the feelings of others. Their intuitive nature means they can become moody or melancholic, drowning in their need to please others and the immense depths of their introspection. When in a bad mood, Pisces may be tempted to stew in their emotions, but they can use their mutable water qualities to explore their spiritual connections to the universe.

CHAPTER FIVE:
ASPECTS AND
TRANSITS

There are several pillars in astrology, and you've already learned how some—like the zodiac signs and the planets—correlate to those signs. There is so much more you can learn about these pillars. When you learn about aspects and transits of the zodiac, you can dig a little deeper into the major parts of astrological readings to account for how planetary bodies change and react in unique ways.

Aspects and transits will each give you more information about yourself and others. They help you keep an active idea of the universe rather than just a stagnant view provided by a birth chart alone. Aspects and transits are two distinct principles, but they work together to give you information, so they are often seen together in astrological books and articles.

Fundamentally, aspects refer to how planets interact with one another and form different geometric formations based on their angles. These angles correspond to the angles between planets based on your natal chart. That may sound quite complicated, but don't worry—you don't need to be an expert in geometry to know how to use aspects.

As you read on, you'll start to realize that aspects aren't too complicated to learn. The more you engage with these parts of astrology, the easier it will be to identify how different geometric concepts relate to your understanding of the universe. Most astrological skills just require practice, and aspects are no exception.

Just like aspects, transits seem outwardly confusing to many beginners, but think of transits as the movement of the planets. A transit occurs whenever a planet's current position creates an aspect with the position of the planet when you were born. As the planetary bodies go through their cycles, each planet will form an angle from where it currently is to where it was in your birth chart.

Different planets have different cycle lengths. For example, Saturn has a cycle that takes 28 years, while the Sun cycles every year. The length of the planets' cycles impacts the type of influence that movement can have on your astrological reading. For example, planets that take longer will correlate with traits and tendencies that are more stable over time, while shorter traveling bodies will change more often.

THE INFLUENCE OF ASPECTS AND TRANSITS

Still a little unclear about why aspects and transits matter? Think about it this way: Just as a bus can move from place to place within a route, the planets can also move between points in the sky. Planets are in different signs at different times, and this impacts several parts of your life. While your birth chart always remains the same, your horoscope can shift based on where the planets currently are in relation to where they were when you were born. Transits change, but they are predictable because the planets follow certain patterns, so astrologers have dedicated methods to find meaning in these components.

Aspects and transits allow the signs to interact, and you can use these characteristics to understand how the distances and degrees between the planetary bodies can impact your present. Planets don't stay in just one place, which means that as they move, the relationships between those planets can shift. Those changes affect your astrological profile and what's going on in your life. Because the geometry of the sky is always changing, staying aware of such changes allows you to go from being just an amateur in astrology to an expert.

COMMON ASPECTS AND TRANSITS

Now that you have a general idea of how aspects and transits work, it's time to put what you've learned into practice to understand the most common aspects and transits that you'll encounter as you practice astrology.

Types of Aspects

Aspects in astrology are often defined as harmonious, neutral, or disharmonious. These types help define how planetary bodies will interact with one another. Harmonious aspects usually work well together, neutral bodies can go either way or interact apathetically, and disharmonious aspects experience tension. The type of aspect isn't necessarily bad or good; it's simply a descriptor to help you interpret what's happening in your chart.

Major Aspects

There are several major aspects that you will need to learn. There are others beyond the ones listed, but in most cases, knowing these major aspects will be enough for you to develop a good understanding of the universe and the zodiac. There are five major aspects that you should keep in mind as you continue your astrological journey.

Conjunction

When there is a 0-degree angle between planets, a conjunction forms. In this situation, it seems like the two planets are on top of one another, but this is just an illusion based on the two planets in correspondence with Earth. During a conjunction, the two planets share a harmonious connection, and the energies of these planets combine.

For example, if a Sun and Gemini are in conjunction, your inherent identity will combine with the ways you act. Thus, a Gemini conjunction between Mars and the Sun results in a person who tends to act in witty and curious ways.

While the formation of conjunctions can be useful because the planets will be on the same page, conjunctions can also create blind spots because it can be hard to distinguish the different parts of yourself. If the Sun is in conjunction with Neptune, your individuality and spiritual selves may feel merged. However, you might not be able to identify the different natures of these parts, which can impact your overall sense of identity.

Opposition

An opposition is a disharmonious aspect that occurs at a 180-degree angle. Opposition creates opposing tension between two bodies, but that isn't necessarily a bad thing as it can often create a lot of energy, motivation, and good results. One of the major areas related to this aspect is relationships. With opposition signs, you may consciously or unconsciously try to find other people who will mirror your experiences.

By connecting with others, those with signs of opposition can find internal harmony and have the opportunity to learn about themselves in the process. Signs in opposition can help you better understand your struggles and discover a conflict within yourself that you might not have otherwise noticed.

When you have signs of opposition, you may be prone to uncertainty and insecurity because you feel like core parts of yourself are antagonistic to one another. However, planets in opposition often share elements. You can reduce this negative tension by reminding yourself to keep an open mind and be open to communication from forces that seem to contradict one another but actually have a lot in common.

Square

A square occurs at a 90-degree angle, and it's another example of a disharmonious aspect. A square aspect can be troublesome because two distinct planets are going in different directions, so it can be hard to reconcile two individual parts that have completely different needs and wants.

Square aspects always demand action to deal with the tension between planets. Most planets in square are going to have incompatible elements, which can make the tension more urgent. However, that doesn't mean you're doomed to internal tension that can't be resolved. In fact, tension can be one of the most motivating forces.

Although planets with a square aspect like to dive into situations, this tendency can cause planets in square to try too much too soon. You may find yourself thrust into a situation that you don't fully know how to handle. However, square aspects help people fight complacency, and as you get older, you learn lessons from mistakes that help you deal with planets in square aspects better than before.

Trine

When two signs form a 120-degree angle, you get a trine. Trines are usually harmonious. The signs work together and can get along, but they aren't blended like they would be in conjunction. Thus, you can more easily distinguish the separation between planets in trine versus those in conjunction.

Trines are a good way to determine what your best talents are because the planets help bring out the best in each other. The talents trines bring out are usually your natural talents, but they don't always represent the talents you are most passionate about improving.

Planets in trine keep a level of separation, but they are neither as enmeshed as planets in conjunction nor as independent as those in sextile. The energy between these planets naturally flows, so you don't have to force a connection. At times, planets in trine may not fully acknowledge the inherent perks of the other planet, but when used together to create constructive outcomes, the planets can find common ground.

Sextile

A sextile happens at a 60-degree angle, and while it's usually harmonious, it can be either disharmonious or neutral when certain planets are included. Sextiles have some similarities to trines because they also relate to your talents. Trines focus on natural talents, while sextiles focus on talents that are burgeoning and exciting. These are talents that you want to spend time improving.

Sextiles generally suggest strong communication and healthy relationships. They direct your energy toward purposes that will help you improve relationships. They allow you to find clarity in what will bring you happiness and discover how to use your relationships and talents to create the best potential outcomes.

Planets in trine can struggle to harmonize with one another at times. It isn't that they don't get along, but they may not fully embrace the cooperation they need to be at their best. However, sextiles can draw upon energy from one another. They often require more conscious awareness to help each planet enrich the other planet in the trine.

Minor Aspects

Beyond just the major aspects, there are also several minor aspects that you should know. The minor aspects aren't completely separate because they're used to subdivide the major aspects. Like the major aspects, these are determined by degrees.

Octile or Semisquare

Octiles, often called semisquares, are 45 degrees and disharmonious.

Trioctile, or **sesquisquares**, are 135 degrees and tend to be disharmonious.

Semisextile are neutral aspects that represent a 30-degree angle.

Quincunx, or **inconjunct**, are neutral at a 150-degree angle.

Quintile are harmonious aspects that come at a 72-degree angle.

Biquintile are 144 degrees and harmonious.

INTERPRETING ASPECTS IN YOUR CHART

Whether you have a lot of certain aspects in your chart or lack those aspects can help you determine what's going on in your life and how you need to proceed.

Lacking Aspects

Looking at what aspects you lack in your chart can help you determine your overall mindset and state.

Conjunctions: You feel scattered, but you are also flexible. When you lack conjunctions, you probably aren't feeling very introspective.

Sextiles: You are feeling uncreative, and you struggle to express and communicate how you're feeling.

Squares: You feel unmotivated, and you don't want to challenge yourself. You likely stay away from conflict and rely on your habits to drive your behaviors.

Trines: You strive to manage conflict, and you're determined to get certain results.

Oppositions: You feel independent, and you don't need a partner to balance yourself out. You are self-reliant and focused on your own view of the world.

Many Aspects

When you have many of these aspects in your chart, you can expect different results.

Conjunctions: You are self-driven, and you look within yourself for answers.

Sextiles: You're creative, and your imagination allows you to express yourself and communicate with other people.

Squares: You act promptly and are good at dealing with crises. Your motivation means you don't mind taking on big tasks.

Trines: You accept how things currently are. You may be talented, but you don't challenge yourself to avoid becoming complacent.

Oppositions: You seek balance in your life by building relationships with others and seeking greater connection to the world around you.

Transits

Transits are like aspects in that they correlate to angles, but they instead represent where bodies are compared to where they once were on your chart. Generally, transits are used in conjunction with your birth chart, but more advanced practitioners can apply transits to other charts like a return or composite chart. You can use your understanding of aspects to also understand transits.

There are so many combinations of transits that can occur based on people's birth charts and how their individual signs interact with one another. Transits are always changing. Thus, you don't need to memorize all the transit combinations. You should be able to understand your own transits by calculating current transits with an online calculator and then using astrological best practices to interpret them.

When evaluating your transits, look at the outer planets first, which are the slower-moving cycles that give you an overview of what you should expect. The outer planets are Saturn, Pluto, Uranus, Neptune, and Jupiter. These planets can take a long time to go through their cycles. Pluto, for instance, takes 284 years to cycle the sun, so it spends anywhere from 12 to 20 years in each zodiac sign. Due to taking so long to pass through the zodiac, outer planets represent broader life patterns.

Once you look at the outer planets, you can then look at inner planetary bodies like Mars, Mercury, Venus, the Sun, or the Moon. The inner planetary bodies affect your daily life more than the outer planets because they move through the zodiac faster. The moon is an example of a planetary body with a short cycle. Every two to three days, it's in a new zodiac sign.

CHAPTER SIX: LOVE AND RELATIONSHIPS

Love and relationships are one of the top areas that people are interested in when learning astrology. These areas of life can be exciting and fun, but they can also include a lot of stress and anxiety. Fear not; while astrology can't make love and relationships easy, it sure can make them easier. Understanding astrological compatibility and how the signs impact your love life or your relationships with friends or family can transform how you connect with other people. This chapter will focus on romantic relationships, but don't worry — all love can fit in here.

Love is a tricky thing to navigate, especially when a relationship is still young. You're dealing with physical attraction while also wondering if the other person is a good fit for you emotionally and socially. Lines can blur between friendship and something more, and with lots of obstacles in every relationship, it's easy to see how knowing if you're compatible with someone is such a big deal. As always, astrology has answers.

Keep in mind that you should never determine whether to start or end a relationship solely based on astrological compatibility. People are complex, which you've probably noticed as you've gone over all the detailed aspects of astrology. Therefore, you can't just assume that a relationship is right or wrong because of a few signs. If anything, astrology should help you navigate challenges in relationships. By understanding the compatibility between you and your love interest, you can figure out ways to address any issues that may arise.

COMPATIBILITY BETWEEN ZODIAC SIGNS

Using sun signs, you can start to understand how each sign will behave in love. Understanding basic love tendencies for each sign is a great way to get started in understanding which ones are compatible. While some pairings have higher compatibility, all combinations have some qualities that can go well together. Plus, there's so much more to consider than your sun sign. In the next section, you will learn how important Venus and Mars can be when considering compatibility.

Aries

By now, you know that those with an Aries sun sign are bold, and this boldness carries through to love lives. If you're looking for a love interest who is direct and clear about their feelings, those with an Aries sign are sure to impress. However, signs who are sensitive may not respond well to those with an Aries sun sign. Aries people can get aggressive, but the right person can bring out their softer side.

Strong romantic connections for Aries include:

- One of the most potentially explosive pairings is Aries and Leo. The fights can get intense with these two, but Aries as a cardinal fire is great at getting projects started, while Leo as a fixed fire helps sustain them.
- Aries and Libra combine action-oriented Aries with balanced, communicative Libra. It can be hard for these two

to let the other take the lead, and Aries's uncompromising nature can frustrate the naturally conciliatory Libra.

- Sagittarius and Aries can have lots of issues because Sagittarians can be so blunt that they can be hurtful. However, Aries is one of the signs that better appreciates a certain level of bluntness. Aries always want to be in charge and struggle to give up control, which can cause conflict.

Taurus

The loyal nature of Taurus makes them a popular choice when it comes to love interests. When a Taurus is committed, they are highly protective of their relationship, but it can take them a while to settle because they want to be sure they're making the right choice and have real feelings for the other person.

Romance often blooms for Taurus with these signs:

- Taurus and Capricorn signs can work quite well in romantic relationships. These two are both grounded due to their earth signs. Thus, they both have practical tendencies. Taurus is loyal and steady, while Capricorn adds ambition to the relationship.
- When you pair a Scorpio and a Taurus, you get a volatile pairing. These two signs are opposites in a lot of ways, but they also bring out the best in each other. Sometimes, opposites really do attract.
- Bring together Taurus and Pisces and you'll get a highly compatible duo. A Pisces sign brings idealism and imagination to the relationship. A Taurus brings their grounded nature. Thus, these two bring out the best in each other.

Gemini

Geminis love to be social, but they also adore intellectual conversations, so they'll want a partner who reflects these tendencies. While they want deep love, they are also flirtatious, so they aren't opposed to casual relationships. It's common for them to fall in love with close friends, and they fall in love quickly, so it doesn't take long for them to be invested.

You'll see Geminis do well in the following pairings:

- Gemini and Pisces are great together when they're at their best, but they need to remember to compromise. Geminis are highly social, while Pisces are more withdrawn and emotional. However, both are open minded and can adjust to the other.
- Libras and Geminis share a lot of positive characteristics because they love trying new things and exploring the world together. This pair is sure to discover new wonders as they learn what makes the other tick.
- When you pair Aries with Gemini, you get a vibrant bond because their fire and air elements can work well with each other. Since Geminis are great at adjusting to whatever situation they're in and are highly social, they are one of the few signs that can keep up with Aries's energy.

Cancer

With deep emotions and an introspective nature, it can be hard to get Cancers out of their shell. While they often want love, Cancers can struggle to take the risk of falling in love because they know that if something bad happens, they'll be devastated. Thus, prospective love interests will need to crack through their armor.

Because they are often homebodies, Cancers love intimate evenings and dinners at home. They're all for lounging around in their pajamas with their sweetheart. They fall in love fast and can sometimes be too giving. Additionally, they can become clingy when they don't feel like they're loved enough.

Some of the top pairings with Cancer are:

- The sensitive Cancer and private Scorpio are great partners because they're both so driven by their emotions. Scorpios need time alone, and as long as Cancers can accommodate that, the relationship can go on strong and each can balance the other out. Both of these partners take a while to open up, but once they do, they're deeply committed to each other.
- Because they are sensitive, Pisces and Cancers go well together because their bond can become super deep. They are both nurturing and affectionate to their partners.
- Virgos and Cancers make an interesting pair because, while Cancers are emotional, Virgos are much more driven by logic. In many ways they are opposite, meaning these two signs can balance each other out.

Leo

Leos aren't often shy. They've got big hearts and expect their romantic interests to love them just as openheartedly. Leos can get hurt when they aren't given enough attention and appreciation for what they do. They're caring individuals, but their need to be the center of attention can cause issues in their relationships. Leos work well with people who understand that Leos are bold and confident people who take pride in themselves and their connections with others.

When Leo meets these signs, relationships will have a lot of excitement:

- Aries and Leo have a bold energy that makes them bring out the lively spirits of one another. However, they can both be a little too passionate sometimes about their own feelings.
- For a couple that's the life of the party, Leos and Geminis fit the bill. They're a blast to be around, and they usually have good banter with one another.
- Pair a Leo with a Sagittarius and you won't regret it. These two are sure to help moderate one another and can bring each other to a delightful middle ground. Sagittarians are full of energy, which meshes well with bold Leos.

Virgo

As the planners of the zodiac, Virgos often see love through a logical lens and can struggle to understand partners who are emotionally driven. However, that doesn't mean Virgos don't have emotional sides they can tap into. Virgos tend to be perfectionists, so their high standards can cross into their romantic lives. They aren't the type to be wooed by grand gestures. They would much rather see their partner's love through pragmatic gifts and practical acts like helping with homework.

Virgos often do best with the following:

- Virgo and Capricorn work well together because they're both earth signs, meaning they are grounded and can be comfortable in a relationship as they strive to build a life together organically.

- While different in many ways, Cancer and Virgo are powerful together because they're so different. It can be hard for these two to understand where the other is coming from because one is logical and the other is emotional. When they get to a place of understanding, they bring out the best in each other.
- If you want a stable relationship, Taurus and Virgo certainly make that happen. Both Taurans and Virgos like stability and are more prone to being logic-driven versus emotionally driven people.

Libra

There's nothing Libras don't love about love. They long for affection and give their love interests tons of it. While love is one of Libras's favorite things, they can be choosy about who they start a relationship with. They want partners who are confident and attractive. Attraction is important to Libras, but what each Libra finds attractive can vary greatly, so while physical attraction is a big part of it, they are far from shallow in pursuit of love.

If you want to know who works best with Libras, consider the following pairs:

- Looking to create balance, Libras connect with Geminis in a mesmerizing way. These two may be indecisive at times, but they're overall on the same page. They both love being around other people and know how to have fun, so they can balance emotional depth and lighthearted times.
- When Capricorn meets Libra, things will likely go well because this pairing creates constancy. One word of caution with this pairing: Libras may get upset when Capricorns

put work ahead of their relationship; Libras will do everything they can to put their relationship first.

- Taurus and Libra also have characteristics that make for a strong relationship. These two are both ruled by Venus, so they share an appreciation for the beauty of the world. They both want loyalty and to make the best of life together.

Scorpio

One of the most intense signs when it comes to love is Scorpio. Scorpios love deeply, and they can become borderline obsessive with their love. They don't hold back and throw themselves entirely into a relationship once they're committed to it. Scorpios take time to let people into their private worlds, but once they do, they expect loyalty from the other person.

The following signs do well with Scorpios:

- Never underestimate a Scorpio and Aquarius pair. While they often need to make compromises to have a long-term relationship, they usually have a strong attraction to one another. However, Scorpios can be too intense, while Aquarians can seem disconnected from the relationship.
- Scorpio and Cancer signs can have an especially deep and meaningful relationship. They both can be clingy, so when they can cling to each other, it works out well. However, throwing two highly sensitive people into a relationship can make it hard for these signs to communicate effectively.
- Get two times the trouble with double Scorpio. When you put Scorpios together, you're going to get one of the most intense and powerful relationships around. Scorpios can work well together because they understand where the

other is coming from and share the same strengths. But watch out—they can be distrustful of one another at first and struggle to be vulnerable.

Sagittarius

Sagittarians are looking for an exciting, fun relationship that's full of energy. They don't commit easily, but that's not because they're insincere. Instead, they want to be sure they're going to end up with the right person. When looking for a love interest, Sagittarians usually search for someone motivated who can keep up with them.

If you're looking to find someone who fits with a Sagittarian, the following are good options:

- While they might seem like a very loud couple, Aries and Sagittarius do quite well together. They both have a lot of energy, and they love to participate in activities. They can get into arguments because of all the energy they have, but they do well when they learn to keep their cool.
- Aquarius and Sagittarius make for a motivated pair because they both live their lives trying to achieve their goals. They love to work together to make their dreams come true.
- The duality of Gemini matches Sagittarius beautifully. However, this relationship is more fun while being less stable. Intellectual debates are common with these two signs. Banter is common because they like to keep things lighthearted, so it may take a while for them to get serious about their relationship.

Capricorn

It takes a while for Capricorns to fall in love, and they often choose to be friends with someone before taking the next step. The slowness of their relationships means that Capricorns build things up gradually, ensuring a strong connection. Capricorns are often career focused and want to ensure financial security. Their love interest will need to understand that Capricorns are already thinking about their future even at a young age.

Capricorns work well with these signs:

- Virgos and Capricorns go together like a dream because they are both highly grounded. They are hard workers who know what they want and won't tolerate anyone standing in their way.
- Bring on the Taurus and Capricorn energy. These two are often on the same wavelength when it comes to values. They make for a reliable couple, and they can easily fall into a comfortable routine together.
- Capricorn times two can be a good pairing. Capricorns work well together because they understand that the other has goals and don't hold one another back. They are also more reserved and communicate what they want.

Aquarius

Aquarians aren't always the most affectionate partners. They can get so invested in trying to make the world a better place that they lose focus of what's happening in their personal lives. Aquarians take their time before getting fully invested. Furthermore, Aquarians love intellectual talks, and talking is one of the ways they feel closest to their love interests.

Aquarians are full of creativity and want to change the world. The following signs can often be found as their partners in crime:

- A double Aquarius pairing can actually work quite well because no one feels hurt when either party is emotionally detached. The relationship can be close, but it can also be more casual without anyone getting too heartbroken.
- A dynamic relationship can be found in Aquarius and Gemini pairings because both signs love intellectual connections. They are also great at social connections. Thus, this pair is full of interconnectivity.
- Libras and Aquarians are ideal matches because they keep each other mentally stimulated and both care about social-justice issues. Both signs want to right things when they are wrong and solve big issues.

Pisces

For Pisces, love feels spiritual. It's part of their drive to find a deeper connection with the world. Pisces use their intuition when looking to connect, and their soulful attempts at love make their partners feel special. Being so gentle and flexible, Pisces can get hurt more easily than other signs, but they still yearn for love.

Some of these signs vibe the best with sensitive Pisces:

Because they are both caring and intuitive, Cancer and Pisces can be good in relationships. They have almost a psychic connection, which makes for deep intimacy.

Scorpios and Pisces bring out a lot of each other's good qualities. They both have deep emotional processes, and they can understand each other's sensitivity and be empathetic to one another.

Pisces and Taurus combine to create a loyal and grounded relationship. Pisces signs can be more emotional and dreamy, but someone with a Taurus sign can help mellow Pisces. Meanwhile, Pisces offer their Taurus lovers more creative and dreamy lives.

IMPORTANCE OF VENUS AND MARS IN RELATIONSHIPS

Have you ever heard the saying, "Women are from Venus and men are from Mars"? Well, there is some astrological truth to this idea because Venus represents the feminine parts of us, while Mars represents the masculine. These two bodies are often highly related to romantic relationships and other bonds. They are great planets to look at if you're curious about your compatibility with another person. This compatibility is most often used for romantic relationships, but it can apply to platonic ones as well.

In astrology, your relationship with Venus and Mars does not necessarily happen on a binary of either man or woman. Accordingly, having feminine energies doesn't make you a woman, just as having masculine energies doesn't make you a man. All people have a relationship with both Venus and Mars, and each person has a balance of feminine and masculine traits. Women, men, and nonbinary people all have parts of each planet within them, and these can show up in many areas of their lives.

For example, one person can have feminine traits like being nurturing while also having traditionally masculine traits like assertiveness. In different circumstances, your traits come out in different ways. You can be assertive when working on a group project at school while being more easygoing at home.

It's no wonder that Venus is so associated with romance; the planet was named after the goddess of beauty and love. Venus is all about love, relationships, and attraction. Whatever sign is in Venus tells us the way we behave in relationships, what qualities attract us, and how we show our love.

Mars, meanwhile, represents the more physical parts of love. Looking at what sign is in Mars can tell you about passion, touch, and what motivates you in relationships.

You can use your Venus and Mars signs alongside others to see if your perspective on relationships and your wants in a relationship align.

Activity: Identify the Venus and Mars Placement in Your Birth Chart and Analyze Their Influence on Your Relationships

Take yet another look at your birth chart. See where your Venus and Mars signs are placed. It's time to analyze how your Venus and Mars signs have impacted your relationships and could impact future relationships. If you're in a relationship, you can also look at the signs of your love interest.

Think about relationships you've had or relationships you want to have. How do you think your signs could impact those relationships? Have your signs ever impacted your ability to form healthy relationships? Consider what your shortcomings and strengths are in relationships, then take some time to think about what you look for most. What kind of people have you gotten along well with? What kind of people do you struggle to maintain relationships with? When you go through these questions, you'll find patterns and start to more deeply understand how you can use astrology to improve relationships going forward.

CHAPTER SEVEN: HEALTH AND WELL-BEING

Just as astrology is commonly used in love and relationships, it's also used frequently in health and well-being. Health is about so much more than your physical health; it also includes your mental and spiritual health. If you want to improve inside and out, you can use astrology to promote well-being and feel better than you've ever felt before. Astrology can't cure health issues or guarantee you'll always be healthy, but it can help you deal with health challenges.

Astrology has a colorful history as part of healthcare, and it has long been used to supplement more traditional forms of medicine. Ancient cultures not only used healers but would also contact astrologers to assist with medical care. Astrologers would help medical professionals get better insight into patients and their conditions. Together, the astrologer and the healer could create a plan that would holistically treat the patient. For example, ancient Egyptians would use charts to figure out the safest times for different medical operations. In medieval times, Europeans used astrological charts for both diagnosis and treatment of their patients.

The use of astrology in medicine decreased in both the 17th and 18th centuries. It was still used, but it wasn't as prominent as a main tool for medical practitioners. The decreased use of astrology in medicine correlated to improved medical techniques and the Age of Reason, when practices like astrology were increasingly considered superstitious. Use continued to decline in the 20th century, but people have become more interested in astrology in the past decade. Society has started to realize that logic and practices like astrology can peacefully coexist and work together to create enriching outcomes.

THE INFLUENCE OF PLANETS AND HOUSES ON HEALTH

Both planets and houses can be used to interpret how astrology connects to health. Each of the planets is associated with health in some way, so being aware of how these planets and houses show up in your astrological readings is a great way to better understand your health.

For each of these planets, you can see how the planet corresponds to various houses in your birth chart or in transit. This information can help you interpret specific information about your health and well-being in general, and you can also predict how your health will be in coming times.

Sun

The sun generally relates to your circulatory system and your heart. Therefore, if you have circulation issues or cardiac problems like heart disease or high blood pressure, this can be related to your sun sign.

Moon

The moon is more related to mental matters and introspection. The shaded nature of the moon means that these issues may not always be illuminated, but they may become outwardly present during certain times of your life. The moon relates to intuition and feelings. Health concerns that can be connected to the moon include depression, anxiety, and other mood issues.

Mercury

Mercury is often related to volatility, which is where the word *mercurial* comes from. Thus, the influence of Mercury can cause moodiness, nervousness, and anxiety. Mercury also relates to your nervous system.

Venus

Those with strong Venus influences may be prone to overindulging while trying to take in the sensory nature of the world. This overindulgence can cause health issues both physically and mentally. Venus influences can also cause people to have weight issues.

Mars

Mars is a high-energy planet. People with big Mars energy can dive so much into things that they physically exhaust themselves. These people need to be careful not to overwork their bodies because doing so can make it hard to recover and lead to bigger health problems down the line. They may also be more likely to have inflammation of various body parts.

Jupiter

Jupiter has a lot of overlap with Mercury since those with strong Jupiter influences may also have issues staying calm. However, Jupiter is also related to growth, so Jupiter can mean going through growing pains, which cause you to have pains that eventually lead to positive self-development.

Saturn

Saturn can be associated with problems like stress. If you feel tense all the time and notice knots in your muscles, that may be related to Saturn placements in your chart.

Uranus

Change and Uranus go hand in hand. Uranus can signal that there are big changes ahead or warn you that you'll go through unexpected health issues. You may not be able to predict what happens to your body, but you can prepare for the unexpected by preparing for it.

Neptune

Those with a lot of Neptune in their charts may find themselves prone to wanting to escape their troubles. This can lead to problems like addiction, depression, eating disorders, or other self-numbing behaviors. Neptune may also cause people to be more prone to dissociating, which feels like having an out-of-body or detached experience.

Pluto

People who have strong ties to Pluto may experience chronic health issues. Specific concerns can either be mental or physical, but they last for a long time and often follow a person through much of their life. The symptoms can wax and wane, and these changes can relate to the movement of the planets, particularly Pluto.

HOUSES

As with any concept, health is deeply related to various houses because astrological bodies are all connected in some way, just as your body is interconnected. However, different houses are related to certain parts of the zodiac more closely, so by looking at certain houses, you can evaluate various parts of your health.

Keep in mind that negative health associations with these different houses don't mean you'll be in negative health or have these consequences. As always, astrology is open to interpretation, so any house can mean a range of things about your health.

First House

The first house is the House of Self, so it's no surprise that it rules over your mind and your head. It also relates to your face. This means that the first house has a lot to do with your mental health and your disposition. Expressions of pain or hurt will relate to this house. If you're having any issues with your head, hair, or facial expressions, the first house may be related. Your vitality is also related to this house.

Second House

Being the House of Possessions, the second house might not seem that related to health at first glance, but this house doesn't just rule over your possessions. It also rules over your self-esteem and self-worth, which is basically like your ownership over yourself. How you feel about yourself highly impacts your health, and research shows that when you have higher self-esteem, you have a drastically higher sense of well-being.

Third House

Your third house is the House of Communication, so it can have a lot to do with your ability to speak your needs and communicate how your body is feeling. However, it also relates to a lot of physical parts of your body. One of the biggest physical functions the third house can impact is breathing. It's also linked to broken bones, cuts, and tumors.

Fourth House

Since it is the House of Home and Family, the fourth house can direct you to familiar struggles and stresses that can weigh on you. It can also help you understand the overall health of your family. If you're dealing with sickness in your family, it may have to do with the fourth house. This house is also related to illnesses caused by hormonal imbalances.

Fifth House

The House of Pleasure, or your fifth house, relates to finding joy in your life and feeling good based on external or internal stimuli. This house is commonly considered "the cure of sickness" because it helps prevent future sickness. The fifth house mostly has to do with stable health and vitality.

Sixth House

The sixth house is one of the biggest houses associated with wellness and health because it is the House of Health. This house is often known for causing diseases, but that is not always the case. This house can give you an overarching idea of your health and wellness. If you're looking for an overview of how well you're doing, look at your sixth house. More specifically, the sixth house relates to organs (including the kidneys).

Seventh House

The House of Partnership is the seventh house of the wheel. This house connects to how diseases spread through a personal connection. Thus, it relates to highly contagious diseases such as COVID-19, measles, or flu. It can also have to do with diabetes, sexual issues, and gland diseases.

Eighth House

Because the eighth house is the House of Sex, Death, and Transformation, it's another one of the top houses used to understand your health. Because of its association with sex, this house can be linked to sexually transmitted diseases. It also has to do with other problems related to intimate areas. Because of its relationship with death, this house can also relate to terminal diseases. Finally, the eighth house can signal extreme mental distress.

Ninth House

Dealing more with your internal processes, the ninth house, or the House of Philosophy, is linked to existential concerns. Thus, it's often related to worry, anxiety, or distress. It can also be connected to physical issues like paralysis, joint issues, and stomach pain.

Tenth House

The tenth house is the House of Social Status, and social status has a lot to do with your health. If you feel out of place in your environment and don't have the social standing you want or the appreciation you need, it can be hard to feel at peace with yourself. For example, if your body looks different from the people around you, this can cause a lot of angst and even lead to you going to extreme means to try to feel better about yourself. Sight issues, joint pain, and stomach pain can also be impacted by this house.

Eleventh House

Your social health is also affected by the eleventh house, the House of Friendship. Your social relationships can help you through tough physical or mental times, and friendship is one of the best ways to promote health. This house often correlates to chronic diseases, but by reaching out instead of keeping to yourself, you can lessen the burden of any chronic condition.

Twelfth House

The last house, the House of the Unconscious, drives all the things that unconsciously impact your health. The twelfth house often relates less to physical issues than the other houses, but it can often be linked to feelings of being trapped or unable to escape your problems. Health problems like insomnia, mental instability, or sorrow can all have to do with the twelfth house.

THE IMPACT OF ZODIAC SIGNS ON HEALTH AND WELL-BEING

Each sign has different areas of health and well-being related to it. Here's an easy list to help you keep track of each sign and its associated parts in order:

- Aries: mind, head, and face

- Taurus: lips, neck, and throat
- Gemini: arms, hands, and lungs
- Cancer: ribs, stomach, and chest
- Leo: heart and spine
- Virgo: lower spine, fingers, spleen, and intestines
- Libra: skin, lumbar area, and kidneys
- Scorpio: bladder, appendix, and nose
- Sagittarius: thighs, hips, arteries, and nerves
- Capricorn: teeth, joints, and knees
- Aquarius: ankles, blood circulation, and legs
- Pisces: lymphatic system, toes, and feet

This list is not exhaustive, but it gives you the main body areas related to each sign. Furthermore, these physical areas can also relate to mental symptoms. For example, if you feel butterflies in your stomach, that can be related to Cancer because of its association with your stomach. If you feel heartache, that may have something to do with Leo.

CHAPTER 8: FORECASTING AND PREDICTIONS

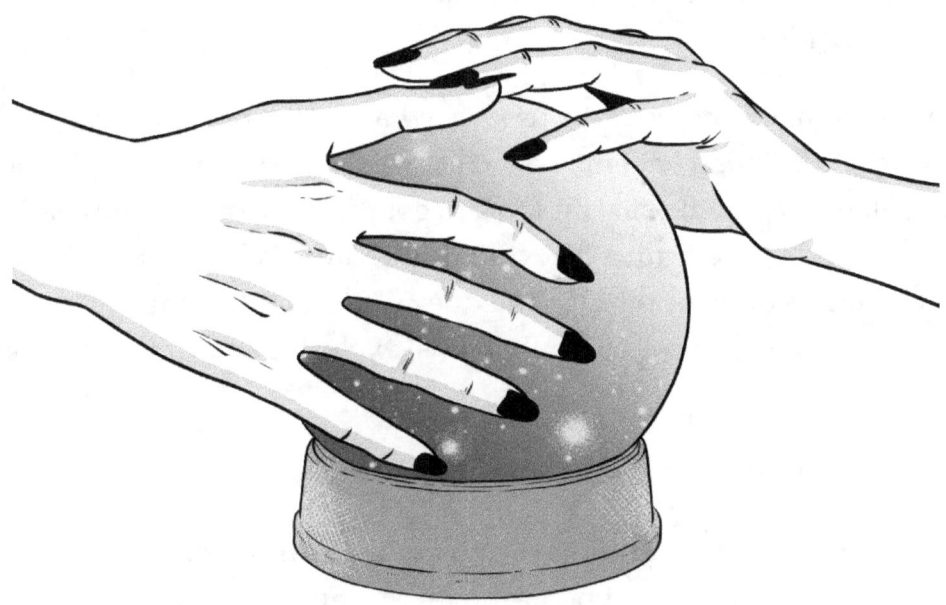

Forecasting and predictions are some of the main reasons that people learn about astrology. Knowing the future is like having a superpower, so it checks out that this part of astrology is especially exciting for newcomers. But how do forecasting and predictions work, and are these accurate ways to understand your future? The answers are a lot more complex than you may think. There are many ways to use astrology for forecasting, but in this chapter, we will focus on the use of transits and progressions.

If you're ready to unpack your future, forecasting and predictions can help you understand what plans the universe may have for you. It's important to recognize that all astrological predictions are guidelines and not guaranteed to happen. While your horoscope may suggest certain likelihoods, you still maintain some control over what happens to you. You always have your free will, and by knowing what tendencies your future may have, you can take steps to mitigate any negatives that may occur and pursue new opportunities.

With so many methods to predict what might happen, you can explore different techniques that work best for you. Most astrologers combine several tools to get the clearest idea of what's happening in the future. They do this because relying on just one technique is often unreliable and doesn't give a full picture of what is going on. With so many unknowns, exploring multiple avenues is helpful.

Some common tools include the following:

- Tracking transits and cycles by monitoring how the planetary bodies move over time
- Adding the analysis of progressions to your understanding of transits
- Looking at outer planets first and then looking for refined predictions with inner planets
- Evaluating the normal cycles of bodies like Mercury, Venus, and Mars in retrograde
- Using solar returns to track when the sun will return to the place of your natal chart

All these areas have significance, but the role of transits and progressions are the most significant. These are the techniques that give the best overall predictive view.

One of the biggest tools you have used so far is your birth chart. Your birth chart gives tons of information, but it isn't the only tool you can use to understand the universe. Your birth chart relates to who you are as a whole person. It represents what you are now and what you will grow into based on the fibers of your being. Progressions, meanwhile, represent how you will develop. This growth plan outlines how you might need to learn new things and adapt. Finally, transits show how events around you influence you. For instance, a traumatic experience can shape your path.

Let's get going and learn how you can use transits and progressions to your advantage.

THE INFLUENCE OF TRANSITS AND PROGRESSIONS

There are plenty of ways that transits and progressions can help you understand the future. Because they deal with how you develop and how events shape you, transits and progressions are most often used when dealing with the future. Birth charts can still give good context into who you are, but focusing specifically on transits and progressions is a great way to understand yourself on a deeper level. They show how people evolve and become more than the circumstances they were born into. Remember that your birth chart continues to have an influence, but it's not the *only* influence.

Imagine you're a cherry tree. Your birth chart represents the seed that will grow into a tree; it defines what type of tree you are and the general mold for what you will be. Your progression defines how you grow as a tree—where your branches reach into the sky and how your blossoms bloom. Despite using the same kind of seed, not all trees grow in the same way. Moreover, situations change how trees grow. This idea is represented in astrology by transits. For example, a big storm can damage a tree or a summer with plenty of rain can help the tree grow strong.

Outer Planet Transits

When using transits, astrologers start with the outer planets, which don't move as quickly around the sun as the inner planets. You can start by understanding where you or another person currently are. Determine how Uranus, Pluto, Neptune, Jupiter, and Saturn are forming aspects with bodies in your natal chart. These aspects can show you how the bodies may be in harmony or disharmony with each other. Outer planets are evaluated first because the transits of these planets have bigger impacts.

Inner Plant Transits

Once you've figured out your outer transits, you can then look at the movement of the inner planets: Sun, Moon, Mercury, Venus, and Mars. You can evaluate these by using aspects based on transits, just as you did with the outer planets. These planets represent smaller changes than the outer planets, so they will refer to less catastrophic changes in your life. Therefore, you may not be as interested in understanding these transits.

Using Secondary Progressions

One of the most common methods that astrologers use regarding progressions is secondary progressions. You can use this method while also using transits to understand your life in different ways. This system relates days to years. For example, the day after your birth correlates to your first year of life. These progressions can give you a year-by-year idea of how your life unfolds. While you can technically use secondary progressions for any planet, it's generally used for planets that move more quickly and relate to key personal concerns.

The planetary signs and planets most used in secondary progressions include:

- Sun
- Moon
- Rising
- Mercury
- Venus
- Mars

The other planets don't change as rapidly, so you won't see them shift as much over time. While you can information from planets like Jupiter, Neptune, Saturn, Pluto, and Uranus, this information is slower to change.

Start by tracking the sun, moon, and rising movement. You can look at the sign and house these bodies are in at any given time. You can also look at any major aspects that may be playing a role, combining the previous knowledge you have learned in earlier chapters.

CHAPTER NINE: ASTROLOGY AND SPIRITUALITY

It's often hard for people to understand how astrology is related to religion and spirituality because that relationship is highly personal and depends on what you believe and how you connect with the world. If you haven't given a lot of thought to your spirituality or don't consider yourself religious, don't worry—this chapter is still for you. Everyone can find a connection to something greater than themselves, and this chapter will help you do that through astrology.

For hundreds of years, astrology and spirituality have been connected. The way they've been connected has changed based on spiritual norms of the times and individual environments; nevertheless, there is no doubt that many people use astrology to improve their spiritual health and find meaning in the world. You can use astrology in that same way too by understanding the spiritual applications of this unique field.

Understanding the Spiritual Aspect of Astrology

Astrology is highly compatible with spirituality, and spirituality is different from religion. You can be spiritual without being religious. Religion focuses on an organized part of spirituality, which includes activities like going to a house of worship, praying, or celebrating traditional sacred events. Spirituality means connecting to your higher power.

Your higher power can be God or another religious being, but it can also be something more abstract like nature, love, or beauty. A higher power is that thing in your life that makes you feel like you are part of something more than yourself. If you don't have a higher power, astrology can help you find one by showing you that the world is so much bigger than yourself.

If you are religious, astrology doesn't conflict with religion. Some might think that astrology is an act of heresy, but it's actually quite aligned with most major religions and echoes many religious values. Astrology is a way of engaging with the universe, and no matter what or who you believe in, astrology can help you find a connection to your higher power.

Wherever you are on your spiritual journey, astrology can be part of that because it allows you to understand yourself and humanity at large. We all want to know about the existence of the world and what our meaning is within it. If you aren't looking for a deeply spiritual practice of astrology, that's okay too, but try to keep your mind open to spirituality when you are practicing astrology. Your spiritual journey may surprise you.

SPIRITUAL PRINCIPLES IN ASTROLOGY

You can focus on your ninth house if you want to learn more about spirituality in astrology. Ruled by Sagittarius, the ninth house is related to philosophy and religion, so it has a lot to do with how you see the world. If the ninth house is a big part of your astrological chart, then religion and spirituality may already be a huge part of your life. If not, you may still want a spiritual connection, but it may be harder for you to process spiritual ideas.

While the third house represents knowledge, the ninth house speaks to a deeper kind of knowledge. This knowledge is the foundation for philosophy and spirituality. By connecting with your ninth house, you can find purpose and meaning in your life even if you're currently struggling to do so.

If you feel a little spiritually lost, don't worry. It's a normal part of life to question what you believe and reevaluate your spiritual identity. Let astrology guide you, and use the ninth house to help you interpret your current spiritual connection. You can then set goals to determine how you want to shape your spiritual self going forward.

By determining what sign is in your ninth house, you can better understand your relationship to spirituality.

Aries

Those with Aries in the ninth house are always looking for new opportunities for spiritual awakening. They love trying new spiritual pursuits and exploring how they can find meaning in the world. At times, people with Aries in their ninth house can be a bit fickle with what gives them spiritual enrichment because they're so eager to explore new areas.

Aries also relates to optimism, so they believe that there are good things out there for them to discover that will produce more alignment with the energies of the universe. The enthusiasm of Aries can be infectious to those around them.

Taurus

People with Taurus in the ninth house are inspired by those who have come before. Tauruses are traditional, and this applies to their spiritual lives as well. They appreciate whatever spiritual practices they are used to. However, loving tradition doesn't mean these people can't explore their spiritual identities. They can
114

embrace some of the traditions they already know while also making room for new traditions.

Because Tauruses are so practical, they may be skeptical about spiritual ideas and resist their spiritual development. It can be helpful for Tauruses to challenge themselves in this area and be more open to spirituality.

Gemini

The pragmatic nature of Geminis carries through to their interactions with the spiritual world. In order to fully embrace the spiritual world, they have to include logic in their spirituality.

Geminis often like to be part of religious organizations because they feel structured and have clearly defined practices. Other Geminis may explore independent spiritual endeavors that more closely align with their sensibilities. For example, Geminis may choose something like science as their higher power, and they may use that concept to drive how they act on a daily basis and how they view the world.

Cancer

Finding calm is one of the main goals of Cancers when seeking spirituality because those with Cancer in the ninth house are acutely emotionally aware. Spirituality often aligns with sensitivity because Cancers are more attuned to the metaphysical rather than the physical.

Although the emotions of Cancers are strong and can change quickly, they are usually pretty consistent with their beliefs because spirituality is so grounding. A lack of spirituality can make these people feel lost and aimless in the world, so finding spiritual development can be transformative.

Leo

When Leos find spiritual awakening, they delve deep into their spiritual lives. They often become leaders in spiritual communities, and their voices are authoritative and trustworthy. They love being around other people, so you often see them actively taking part in religious events rather than favoring solo spiritual endeavors.

Leos can be a little controlling in their passion to create a strong spiritual community, but they are good at sustaining spiritual projects and bringing new life to religious communities.

Virgo

Virgos are hard workers, so they'll find spiritual pursuits that speak to their work ethic. They don't like to just sit back and watch, and they want to be in the weeds, striving to create projects.

Due to their rational nature, Virgos like a more systematic approach to spirituality. They prefer hard facts to abstract principles. Virgos are articulate, so speaking about their spiritual beliefs is a perfect way for them to engage. The worldview of Virgos is highly reliant on careful analysis and established events and facts about the world. Virgos are open to new ideas, but it'll take some convincing if you want to sway someone with Virgo in the ninth house.

Libra

Those with Libra in the ninth house love to find harmony in the world, so their spiritual beliefs are often related to things that bring balance to the world. They love their spiritual beliefs to feel fair and just to all people.

Libras love intellectual conversation, so having deep spiritual talks is appealing. They only want to engage with people who they know will give them the rewarding conversation they crave. Libras will find beauty in the world through their spirituality, and they will use cultural pursuits like art or music to further connect to their spiritual ideas.

Scorpio

Philosophy is a core part of those with their ninth house in Scorpio. These people often grow into their religious beliefs, and as they get older, they start to become more spiritual as they ask questions and aim to make sense of the world. The meaning of existence is important to Scorpios, and it keeps them curious as they grow older.

Those with Scorpio in the ninth house love to connect with their spiritual beliefs by asking questions and challenging their current understanding. Scorpios strengthen their faith and are fueled by positive discourse. However, they may be more reluctant to open up about their beliefs with people they don't know as well because Scorpios can be quite private.

Sagittarius

If you have Sagittarius in the ninth house, you probably love spiritual bodies that have already been established. These people know that community is a great way to find spiritual enrichment, and they are strongly motivated by their community's moral guidelines.

These people embrace the mystery of the world, which encourages them to explore what they don't know. They are okay if they don't have all the answers because they love the process of searching and exploring possibilities. Spirituality is about the journey and all the wonderful things that can be found along the way.

Capricorn

People with Capricorn in the ninth house are more conservative in their spiritual practices than some of the other signs, meaning they are drawn to traditional spiritual systems and hesitant to explore new practices.

Capricorn in the ninth house means that people are driven toward their purpose. They want to fulfill what the universe has in store for them, and the goal is to become consistent in their practices.

Aquarius

Having Aquarius in the ninth house means that a person has progressive and bold views of the world. These people often like to fight against the status quo and find new meaning in ordinary things. Aquarius signs take existing spiritual beliefs and turn them on their head to understand them better.

These people don't want to be like everyone else, and social justice is often an important part of their spiritual processes. They are also highly sociable, so you'll see Aquarians excitedly sharing their beliefs with others. They speak intellectually and with so much moral enthusiasm that they can be quite convincing in their beliefs.

Pisces

Those with their ninth house in Pisces are sure to be highly curious about spiritual matters because it speaks to their core sense of self and intuitive nature. The ninth house in Pisces can indicate an intuitive and almost psychic connection to the universe or at least a yearning toward that level of connection. People with this placement may also want to try intense spiritual practices like astral projection.

If your ninth house is Pisces, it's likely that you want to spiritually develop because you long to understand why the world is what it is. Your focus is on the questions that can't be answered by science alone and those that speak to more mystical matters of the universe.

CHAPTER TEN: ETHICS IN ASTROLOGY

Ethics is a field that seeks to understand moral principles that overarch various areas of our lives, and most areas of study or work have some kind of ethical standards. Ethics ensures that people in areas like medicine, science, and astrology abide by moral standards. Keeping these ethics in mind will be important as you develop your practice of astrology. By choosing to practice astrology, you must also hold yourself to an ethical standard.

In the area of astrology, the International Association of Ethics in Astrology (IAEA) ensures that astrologers act appropriately in their behaviors, practices, and standards. The IAEA includes astrologers from different traditions of astrology and helps spread awareness of ethical astrological practice. In this chapter, you will learn some of the most important aspects of ethical astrology so that you are always responsible in your practice and don't do more harm than good.

There haven't always been firm ethical standards in place in astrology, and this meant that practitioners could abuse their positions and give inaccurate or harmful information. Especially when people weren't as aware of the intricate details of astrology, certain practitioners could easily exploit that ignorance. For example, when astrology was widely used in medicine, astrologers could influence whether a person lived or died.

Fortunately, the stakes are no longer as high. Plus, more information is widely available, so more people are on guard when given astrological information. However, that doesn't mean people aren't still susceptible to lies or manipulation. Ethics evolve as humans prioritize different values. You should strive to uphold modern ethics and values that permeate today's culture rather than looking to past ethical standards.

Understanding the Importance of Ethical Practices in Astrology

Ethics in astrology is important because it guarantees that no one takes advantage of other people or treats them irresponsibly. When dealing with people's bodies or minds, ethics are even more important, and astrology is often an intimate experience. Having ethics can protect people from getting unnecessarily hurt.

While astrological standards are often set specifically for professionals who do readings for other people, these principles are also useful for people who are practicing on their own or giving readings to friends and family.

Astrology should never be used to intentionally harm or upset other people. Focus on the positive elements of astrology, and you will have a much better connection with the practice and feel good about yourself.

COMMON ETHICAL CONCERNS IN ASTROLOGY

The following tips outline steps you can take to avoid major ethical breaches that can result in a situation where someone is hurt. As you continue to practice your astrological skills, you should also practice ethical skills.

Respect Other Astrological Traditions

Not all astrologers will use the same techniques and traditions to inform their practice, and that doesn't mean anyone is wrong. It just means that all astrologers approach the world and try to understand it in unique ways. Just as different schools have different classes, astrologers have their own focus areas as well. Always respect the beliefs of others while still being passionate about your own beliefs.

When you're respectful of other astrological traditions, you not only give other people the compassion they deserve, but you also give yourself the chance to learn more. Even if you never subscribe to other astrological traditions, you can certainly learn how to be a better astrologer by seeing how other practitioners work. Keeping an open mind allows you to expand your knowledge and perspective. You may even find that other traditions appeal to you or that you want to borrow from other traditions to create an eclectic practice.

Remember that astrologers have more in common than not. We're all just trying to understand how the heavens above relate to our lives. The more people who explore astrological practice, the better. It doesn't matter how they decide to structure that practice. Just as all families have different traditions, different astrologers do too, and that diversity makes astrology beautiful.

Do No Harm

Never use astrology as a weapon or to mess with someone's head. When you give other people astrological readings, you have a level of responsibility to act with compassion and care. Astrology should be never used to manipulate or exert power over another person. Astrology can influence people's behaviors and perceptions of the world and themselves, so you must not harm others with this powerful practice.

When you choose to practice astrology, never forget that when people are seeking answers, they are vulnerable. This vulnerability can be a wonderful way to find a connection in the world, but bad actors can take advantage of people's vulnerabilities and use them for monetary or other personal gain at the expense of others.

Even if your intentions are never to do harm, it's possible to unconsciously act in harmful ways. The ethical standard is that you should take steps to reduce harm as much as possible. Nevertheless, remember that it's impossible to control human emotions. Astrological information can hurt people even when you don't intend to do so and have done everything in your power to act responsibly. If that happens, it doesn't mean you've done anything wrong. It just means that you should try to be more aware of how people around you are reacting. As long as you're making a conscious effort not to hurt people, you're following this principle.

Be Honest About What You Can Do

Never lie about your capabilities, and remember that you're still only human. Astrology will never make you omniscient, and you should never insist you have skills you don't have. Be clear with other people and yourself about the things you can and cannot know using astrology to avoid creating unrealistic expectations. Unrealistic expectations are bound to lead to negative feelings, and they sour the experience of astrological practices.

Always keep in mind that astrology is never an end-all-be-all practice. There's no way any human can confidently assert that they know exactly what the future will hold because there are so many variables we simply can't calculate or even understand. Astrology can't define someone's future, and you can't understand a full person without getting to know them beyond whatever their chart says. Astrology is a rough sketch, not the finished picture. Free will allows us to make decisions that can change or shift our fates or tendencies, so make it clear to other people that astrology should give them clarity, but it doesn't provide all the answers.

Understand How Your Actions Impact Others

Always think about how your actions can influence other people. If you're likely to do more harm than good, it's probably best to change your course and act with care instead. This ethical principle includes the idea that you should be aware of how astrology can be used to help people. You can do good, so when you see the chance to do so, try to find joy through sharing astrology with others.

Astrology is a huge responsibility, so it can be a challenge to learn the impact you'll have right away. Don't be too hard on yourself if you make a mistake along the way. Instead, learn from those mistakes. Mistakes are a great way to grow and do better in the future.

You can do a lot of good with astrology, and that's such a cool ability to have, so embrace that ability to the fullest. Whenever you can, spread some goodness into the world. Sharing your talents can be highly rewarding and make you feel a sense of fulfillment and a higher purpose. It can also help you build a rich astrological community.

CHAPTER ELEVEN: CONCLUSION

You've done a lot of work to get to this point, and while it's time to wrap things up, your relationship with astrology is far from over. The knowledge you've learned can continue to impact you and give you wisdom and connection to the world around you.

Important Concepts in Astrology for Teens

Many concepts have driven the astrological study in this book. These concepts are ones that you will want to continue to use and practice. If you need to review anything, you can always go back through the pages of this book to refresh.

You've been introduced to the truths and myths of astrology. The history and continued relevance of astrology speak to its universality and application to people of all types. You've seen how astrology has influenced human thought and advancement and continues to align with many values people still hold dear.

Furthermore, you learned what zodiac signs, planets, and houses are in astrology; how they can be used; and what your birth chart means. Your chart may have started as something overwhelming and confusing, but now you can make big steps to interpret it. With continued practice, it will give you even more answers.

With careful study, you discovered the differences between your sun, moon, and rising signs. These are the main signs that are used in astrology, and while they aren't the only ones, they're a great way to get a broader understanding of yourself and the world without having to go too far into the weeds.

This book taught you the value of elements and modalities, which will allow you to further classify the signs and understand their more nuanced natures. Elements and modalities help you see the signs in new ways, and they connect individual signs with others that share some of the same characteristics. This connection helps you see how the planetary bodies work together in complex but beautiful ways.

The beauty of the sky can also be seen in aspects and transits, which have become an influential part of how you understand your birth chart and the movement of astrological bodies. Your astrological study cannot just include your static birth chart, but to understand your future, you must also embrace how planetary bodies move dynamically and bring new meaning over time.

Additionally, you now understand how astrology can be used for love and relationships. Whether you're in a relationship or you're just starting to understand your romantic side, astrology can show you how to make your relationships better and stronger, regardless of the challenges you may face on your love journey. Love is hard, but astrology can alleviate some of those struggles.

Astrology can also be used to promote health and well-being, which we all need a little more of in our lives. Your mental and physical health are so interconnected to the sky, but they are too often neglected, especially when nothing seems wrong.

Health and well-being are important, but what most people want most is to understand their future. You can now embrace astrology as a tool to learn more about your future. No one can know exactly what will happen, but they can understand possibilities by using various predictive methods that serve as a guide rather than a definitive map.

Astrology hasn't just touched your future; it has also touched your soul. Even if you aren't religious, astrology can be deeply spiritual and connect to your higher power, whatever that power may be. Finding your higher power is one of the best ways to explore who you are and what you want from your life, and through astrology, you can more easily discover who you are.

Finally, you learned how important ethics are in astrology and how to maintain appropriate ethics when practicing astrology. Being responsible about how you use your skills will ensure that no one gets unnecessarily hurt through astrology and that all practitioners are held to a certain ethical standard that makes the practice better.

These lessons have given you the tools you need to reach your goals and find your purpose in this chaotic world. You can now go out into the world with more confidence and joy. Astrology is not an easy skill to learn, but it is well worth the effort you will put in.

Tips for Continued Learning and Development in Astrology

Feeling a little lost about where you want to go on your astrological journey? Well, there's no need to stress. Here are 10 tips you can use to continue developing your astrological knowledge and practical skills:

- Practice daily. The more you practice, the better your skills will get.
- Find astrological friends to find more satisfaction in your practice by sharing it with others.
- Set goals. Having goals gives you a clear path forward and an understanding of what you want.

- Pay more attention to the world rather than ignoring all the wonders around you, which can give you a sense of fulfillment.
- Let your practice evolve. People change over time and must let their astrological practice reflect those changes.
- Try new techniques to challenge your skills and show yourself that you can always learn more.

These simple steps will take your astrological development in exciting directions and help you explore the parts of astrology that give you the most fulfillment.

SELF-REFLECTION AND MINDFULNESS IN ASTROLOGY

Astrology isn't just about understanding the way the planetary bodies move. In order to be good at astrology, you also have to foster an overall strong sense of self and both physical and mental wellness. Self-reflection and mindfulness are powerful tools that will not only help you in your astrological practice but will also apply to other areas of your life as well. These tools are mostly gained through practice and consciousness, which you will learn more about as part of your commitment to astrology.

Self-reflection allows you to be honest about your role in the world and how your astrological information applies to you. To self-reflect, you must look inward and be honest about who you are, what you want, and what struggles you're up against. When you can't self-reflect, it's usually because you're focused on outside forces rather than yourself.

You can self-reflect by completing the following:

Pay attention to what's happening right now: Mindfulness will help you with this task. Consider your feelings, what's going well in your life, and what's going badly. Astrology can help you understand your future, but don't forget to understand your present.

Think about what you most want: Consider the things that you most want in your life. Detach your wants from the wants of other people around you. It's okay to have input from other people, but don't let yourself be defined by what your family members, teachers, or friends may want for you. Knowing what you want is one of the biggest goals of self-reflection.

Journal: Journaling is a great way to self-reflect because it allows you to process your feelings and more easily cope with whatever is going on in your life. Research has shown that the self-reflection related to journaling can make you both happier and healthier.

Always grow: No matter how old you get, there's always more to learn about the world and you'll have to evolve as things in your life change. Stay aware of the changes and growth opportunities you have. The stars aren't always in the same places, and that's okay.

Remember that you aren't alone: To understand yourself, it helps to look at yourself through the lens of other people.

What role do you play in other people's lives? How does the universe connect you with those people through the planetary bodies?

Find joy in nature: Astrology is all about appreciating the deeper meaning of the universe, and that doesn't mean just understanding the planetary bodies above. You also have to be aware of how you connect to the natural world. Take a walk outside or appreciate some fresh air at the park. Finding small ways to appreciate nature can help you reflect more clearly on your relationship with the universe.

Disconnect for a while: Most of us are somewhat attached to our phones and other devices. It's hard to be away for them for any amount of time, but finding time to unplug, even if it's just a few moments, can help you be in tune with yourself without as much external distraction.

Mindfulness is all about being present and accepting the stars as they are. You must learn to be present and not get too caught up in either the past or the future. Take time to be aware of what you are doing and how you are feeling. You can do this by journaling, meditating, and just letting your thoughts be without judgment. Mindfulness can apply to any area of your life, and trying to instill mindfulness in as many areas as possible can help you create a mindset that's optimal for astrological study.

The best ways to get started on your mindfulness journey are:

Understanding that you are not your thoughts: A key to being mindful is separating your thoughts from who you are. We all have negative thoughts, but those thoughts never have to correlate to our actions. Your astrological

133

chart can say a lot about you and your tendencies, but it can never define what you do; that's all up to you. Bad thoughts don't make you a bad person, just as good thoughts don't make you a good person.

Journaling: Journaling helps with self-reflection, but it's also one of the greatest tools you can use to be mindful. When journaling for mindfulness, consider more than just who you are. Process what you feel about the external world. A journal is a great place to go over all the information you learn from astrology and keep a log of how the planets move and how that has impacted you.

Meditation: You may think of meditating as sitting with your legs crossed or practicing yoga, but it's so much more than that. Meditating helps you control your breathing so that you can venture into your own mind with curiosity and no judgment. Astrology calls for you to keep an open mind, and as you learn to meditate, you'll also learn to process the world around you without presumptions that may be wrong.

Knowing your patterns: Be mindful of your habits because your habits often define how you behave. Habits are things that you do without conscious thought. You complete habits because you're used to them. When you make habits conscious, you can change or embrace them. This concept applies to astrology because astrology defines your patterns and tendencies, and by understanding those parts of yourself, you can react in positive ways.

Let go of what was and what will be: Thinking about the past or the future isn't a bad thing, but it shouldn't prevent you from being present in the current moment. The past and future have a role in your life, but you must let go of your need for control. You can't change what's already happened or dictate what's coming next, so there's no reason to try.

Accepting what is: Your situation right now is something you can influence, but if you aren't where you'd like to be, there's no point in fixating on your unhappiness. Instead, learn to appreciate what you can do right now. Take in your feelings and let them be whatever they are. Accepting what is doesn't mean you cannot plan for the future or aspire to greater things. It just means that you need to accept your situation whether you like it or not.

You need to have both self-reflection and mindfulness if you want to succeed at astrology. Both concepts are interconnected. Self-reflection helps you be more mindful, and mindfulness helps you be more self-reflective. These concepts can be a challenge, but with time and practice, you can make them a profound part of your life and these skills will benefit your astrological practice.